The *GREAT* CLAM CAKE *and* FRITTER GUIDE

The *GREAT CLAM CAKE* and *FRITTER GUIDE*

Why We LOVE Them, How to MAKE Them, and WHERE to FIND Them from MAINE to VIRGINIA

CAROLYN WYMAN

Globe
Pequot

Essex, Connecticut

For Velveeta the cat (2011–2022)

Globe
Pequot

An imprint of Globe Pequot, the trade division of
The Rowman & Littlefield Publishing Group, Inc.
4501 Forbes Blvd., Ste. 200
Lanham, MD 20706
www.rowman.com

Distributed by NATIONAL BOOK NETWORK

British Library Cataloguing in Publication Information available

Library of Congress Cataloging-in-Publication Data available

ISBN 978-1-4930-6587-5 (paper : alk. paper)
ISBN 978-1-4930-6588-2 (electronic)

∞™ The paper used in this publication meets the minimum requirements of American
National Standard for Information Sciences—Permanence of Paper for Printed Library
Materials, ANSI/NISO Z39.48-1992.

Contents

Acknowledgments

I wanted to write a clam cake book long before the pandemic. But with most clam fritters being sold at summer-only outdoor stands, it turned out to be the perfect book to research during it. Thanks to Michael Steere's steering me to Amy Lyons of Globe Pequot and Amy's enthusiastic "Let's do it!" I was able to spend the better part of two pandemic summers by the water eating delicious food and talking to some fascinating people.

At least the pandemic was a perfect time for me. With COVID-related supply shortages and help almost impossible to find, it was far from an ideal time for clam shack owners to sit around and chat. That they did anyway makes this book possible, and I am forever grateful. Special shoutouts to Elsie Foy of Aunt Carrie's, David Gravino and Lynn DeSouza of Iggy's, Denise Gelinas of Huot's, Kevin Durfee and Yulia Kuzmina of George's, and Todd Blount and Patricia Gaudreau of Blount Clam Shacks for graciously responding to multiple questions and requests.

This book was a homecoming for this native Rhode Island junk food historian and double the usual pleasure (and half the cost!) in putting together because of the time I was able to spend with Southern New England-based friends and family while reporting. Among those who provided a place to rest and respite from my clam cake diet were my brother Vern and the other Rhode Island Wymans (both two- and four-legged), cousin Linda and uncle Mick Tillson, and longtime friends Phil Greenvall and Ana Silfer. This book also benefited from Vern's tips, ex-boss Rudi Hempe's Rolodex, Cynthia Heininger's cooking, Kate LeBlanc's research, nephew Jim Wyman's photography, and husband Phil Blumenkrantz's support and counsel.

Though I ate clam cakes through most of my youth and early adulthood, I didn't appreciate the dish's complexity and long history in Southern New England until I began work on this book and examined the work and/or racked the living brains of authors, historians, preservationists, collectors, and clam cake makers that came before, especially Sandra Oliver, Kathy Newstadt, Ed Serowik, Felicia Gardella (of the Warwick Historical Society), John Howell (of the Rocky Point Foundation), David Bettencourt, Bruce Remick, Donald Wyatt, Tom DeCosta, Greg Pecchia, Bob Rodericks, Mike Urban, Brooke Dojny, Elizabeth Bougerol, Sarah Schumann, Keith Stavely and Kathleen Fitzgerald, and Chris Martin and David Stone.

Thanks are also due the Free Library of Philadelphia's Interlibrary Loan Department and Renee Pokorny of that library's South Philadelphia branch for procuring and delivering almost any obscure volume I hungered after; and to Thomas Frawley of the North Kingstown (RI) Free Library, Erica Luke of the South County History Center, and the Providence (RI) Public Library, especially Kate Wells and Angela DiVeglia of its Rhode Island Collections, for access to 1800s travel guides and photos invaluable to this book's first chapter.

Although I was born with a RI clam cake in my mouth, I started this book knowing little about the clam cake and fritter traditions in Maine, Virginia, and North Carolina. And I would still know next to nothing but for books and papers like *A South You Never Ate* by Bernard Herman and "Living on the Edge" by Jennifer J. Edwards, and the time and patience afforded me by Rodney Laughton, Andy Linton and daughter Andi-Kay Tyler, Emily Machen, Wendy Robertson, Dave Mallari, Sean Fate, Karen Colvin, Brian Casey, and others quoted or cited herein.

Finally, and most importantly, I'd like to thank the residents of Rhode Island, Maine, Virginia, Massachusetts, Connecticut, and North Carolina whose love and continued patronage of clam cakes and fritters have kept this nineteenth-century treat alive for our enjoyment into the twenty-first century and, hopefully, beyond.

Introduction

America's restaurant tables are groaning with hamburgers, hot dogs, pizza, chicken fingers, and tacos.

That is unless you find yourself at a shack near the water in Southern New England, Virginia, and Maine, places where a historic plethora of clam beds and a longtime love of fried foods have come together to create a love for dishes variously known as clam cakes or clam fritters.

Funfetti cake with clam bits subbing for colorful sprinkles just pop into your head? Then you must be from some other place and in need of insider advice.

Here's mine: Forget Mystic Seaport, Plimoth Patuxet, and the Jamestown Settlement. If you want to experience living history of the most delicious kind, go to a clam shack and order clam cakes or fritters.

In Maine, that will get you a deep-fried clam patty with a soufflé-like center; in Virginia, a clam-filled pancake; and in Rhode Island, clam-flavored doughnut holes purchased by the dozen or half-dozen and consumed communally by bare hands as part of a statewide sacred summer ritual.

How big is this dish in America's smallest state?

The cakes are among the top two or three sellers at virtually every clam shack in Rhode Island, a favorite metaphor (a stupid person being "just shy of a dozen clam cakes"), and, paired with chowder at free luncheons, are the best way for a RI politician to cozy up to constituents. In the scary, early pandemic lockdown days, some Rhode Islanders actually risked their lives to stand in line to get clam cakes at Iggy's, prompting an exasperated then-RI Governor (now US Commerce Secretary) Gina Raimondo to scold, "Knock it off!"

In fact, you might say clam cakes made Rhode Islanders what they are today, which is heavy, imperfectly shaped, greasy-fingered, and dotted with brown spots from a too-longtime bouncing around in nature's fryolator (i.e., the water) on a sunny day, like their favorite fried treat.

I can say this because I'm a native Rhode Islander who grew up eating clam cakes at Crescent Park and Rocky Point amusement parks and at oceanside clam shacks to their south. But it was only after moving away and writing books about Spam and the Philadelphia cheesesteak that I remembered the equally fun fatty food of my youth that was equally deserving of book exploitation/examination.

This book makes up for that oversight while simultaneously giving me a tax-deductible excuse to spend a summer lounging around beautiful seacoast settings stuffing my face with delicious seafood.

While I was stuffing my face, I also stuffed my brain with incredible stories of "boat person" Phuong Lam's harrowing escape from Communist Vietnam to fame as Worcester, Massachusetts's clam-fritter-making Egg Roll Lady;

of the owners of Flo's Drive-In, who have survived multiple hurricanes with humor still intact (judging from their "Closed hurricanes" sign); and of Hank's and Evelyn's, clam-shacks-turned-community-gathering spaces, offering free concerts or benefit fundraisers.

Or Deary Brothers, Beach Pub, and the 100-plus-year-old Woodman's, places that are as much a source of family history and pride as they are of cakes and fritters.

I learned the tricks of the clam-cake-making trade shared in Chapter 4 standing by the side of the masters at Aunt Carrie's and Martha's Kitchen, survived the lines at Huot's and Iggy's, and fought valiantly for my right to lunch with seagulls almost everywhere.

Is your favorite clam cake stand missing? It could be because your place makes better clam fritters than a story. Or maybe they were still on my list of to-dos when my doctor issued her cease and desist order due to my cholesterol count. I did actually physically go to the places here-profiled (and some others, making bad cakes, here-omitted), unlike most of your Internet best-of list compilers. But write me nicely (don't begin, "Dear Idiot"), and your favorite could end up in a future edition.

One reason these stands are so interesting: There is, as yet, no big multi-state chain restaurant selling clam cakes. The bad news for those hoping to enjoy this food somewhere besides a picnic bench while wearing a wet bathing suit: There are no high-end restaurants selling clam cakes either, not even high-end seafood ones.

Clam cakes have always been an everyman and everywoman food; they are typically the cheapest seafood dish on the menu. That's because it's made of little chopped-up or minced pieces of the toughest clams, extended with flour, and sometimes a little cornmeal, or (in Maine) crackers.

The Rhode Island-style clam cake, in particular, is a dough ball that is merely flavored by clam juice and a few clam pieces, which, by the way, most locals are fine with if the dough is not greasy or a gut-ball/sinker (so heavy that it immediately sinks to the bottom of your stomach). Though, lack of clams *is* a common complaint of tourists and other first-timers. (So, if you don't want to be pegged as a know-nothing outsider, knock it off!)

While featuring the bivalve that has defined East Coast Americans, and especially New Englanders, for generations, cakes and fritters present the clam in a form that is much easier to swallow than steamers or fried clams with their squishy, strongly flavored bellies. Yet they're also deliciously fried, in some places, with lard. Lard, here in the health-conscious twenty-first century! A few makers even boast of this, and rightly so, because nothing tastes better. And it's not like you're eating at a clam shack every night, right?

That brings us to the final and most important reason people love clam fritters: They're only of a certain wonderful time and place. Originally, as detailed in this book's first chapter, they were fried up by mom or grandmom at home, at shore resorts in New England that morphed into amusement parks that are still remembered fondly by living Rhode Islanders; or at fundraising carnivals in Virginia that still take place. And now also and chiefly at seasonal, waterfront restaurants and shacks that people frequent on vacation.

An August 1973 family beach picnic: an enduring memory

Mention clam fritters to most people in their East Coast hot spots and what you'll get back are memories of chowing down on cakes and chowder with family and friends at big, long communal tables at Rocky Point, pulling a hot, crispy one out of a grease-stained bag at the beach, or grabbing one of grandma's fritters off a platter at a Fourth of July picnic spread.

Like these memories, the clam cake/fritter-eating experience is fleeting. A fritter is best the first few moments after it's fished from the fryer or pan.

Here's hoping dwelling on this food with me will bring these memories to mind and prolong the pleasure long after the last bite of clam-flavored cake is gone.

CLAM CAKE V. FRITTER

Are they clam cakes or clam fritters? Yes, and yes. And do the two terms refer to the same dish? Sometimes.

Nowadays, most Rhode Islanders call their beloved clam-flavored balls clam cakes. Although that was not always the case. Historically, they were also, less frequently, called clam fritters. For instance, storied amusement park Crescent Park and clam cake restaurant Aunt Carrie's both called them clam cakes and clam fritters at various points in time—in a few cases, interchangeably on different areas of the same menu. But questions from diners about what they were serving caused Aunt Carrie's to switch to the more locally common "cake" in the early 1980s.

Most—but not all—clam shacks in Connecticut and Massachusetts call these same clam balls fritters.

Got it? No? It gets worse.

Fried clam patties are called clam cakes in Maine and clam fritters in the shoreline communities in Maryland, Virginia, and North Carolina.

This book wishes to leave etiological discussions of the terms fritter and cake and their accuracy when applied to these clam dishes to the owner of the Hitching Post (see p. 59). We will instead endeavor to follow current social conventions in honoring stands' right to name their own creations. In general discussions, we will follow the general regional naming conventions referenced earlier.

Should you ever make the mistake of uttering the phrase "clam fritter" in front of a fanatical native Rhode Islander (and I'm sorry, it *will* almost certainly be a Rhode Islander), do not engage. Just nod and smile, running that famous saying about a clam cake called by any other name being just as good over and over again in your mind.

And remember: This story is here to reference if you get confused.

1
DIGGING INTO CLAM CAKE AND FRITTER HISTORY

Rhode Island is a little state of big eaters. In few other places is the love of food so great, the culinary customs so numerous, and the portion sizes so enormous. Rhode Island culinary excess peaked in the huge seafood feasts served after the Civil War at summer resorts ringing Narragansett Bay, which simultaneously sealed Southern New England's love of the clam cake.

Out of an eating marathon that also often included lobster, corn on the cob, and clam chowder, the dish that survived to define Rhode Island into the twenty-first century is clam-flavored doughnut holes. It's a truth easier to swallow when you know that the mid-nineteenth-century shore dinner menu also could include fried eel, stewed liver, clam drink, and scup.

Today native New Englanders and visitors alike stand in line for hours in the hot summer sun to score a half-dozen clam cakes and other fish favorites, as the profiles in this book's next chapter convincingly attest.

But this love is relatively recent.

"The aboundance of Sea-Fish are almost beyond beleeving," reported the Reverend Francis Higginson upon arriving in New England in 1629. But for the most part, the Pilgrims and other early white settlers could have cared less. They were much more interested in eating the kinds of protein they had back in England, which is to say beef. Among the many issues the Pilgrims had with fish: It was not filling, spoiled quickly, and had bones that sometimes required removing from the mouth while eating, "a socially awkward activity," argues Sandra Oliver in her early American seafood history book, *Saltwater Foodways.*

Clams were especially hated. The Pilgrims fed them to their pigs and only ate clams themselves in times of extreme deprivation. Recalled Massachusetts Bay Colony Governor John Winthrop of a period of crop failure: "Many families in most towns had none to eat, but were forced to live off clams, muscles [mussels], . . . dry fish, etc."

Procuring clams also required these former middle-class merchants and tradesmen—or, more accurately, their wives—to muck about in the mud like their "uncivilized" Native neighbors, another negative. In his 1653 history *Wonder-Working Providence*, Edward Johnson describes "the soules" of these women clam diggers rejoicing at the sight of two provision ships from Ireland as Christ "manifest." Though Johnson doesn't say what happens next, it's easy to imagine the women throwing down their clam baskets and running toward the promise of their preferred beef.

New England Native Americans baked or steamed their clam catches, judging from the piles of shells or middens uncovered by archeologists. And they reserved some of the prettiest clamshells to make wampum beads, which were used as both ceremonial wear and currency, they were that prized. But if the colonists baked clams, it's not likely something Indigenous people taught them, Kathy Neustadt argues pretty convincingly in her 1992 study, *Clambake*.

The New England colonists did finally find value in their vast fish resources—especially cod—as a trading commodity to fish-loving Roman Catholic countries like Portugal and Spain. Clams first found their commercial value as bait to catch the cod. Lesser-quality fish was sold in the West Indies to feed the slaves as part of the infamous triangular trade that made New England a center of rum production.

Neustadt says Americans only developed an appetite for clams and clambakes much later. It was part of a nostalgic reimagining of how well the Pilgrims adapted to their new homeland as part of Plymouth-Rock-landing commemorative celebrations in 1720 and afterward. Some of these "forefather" dinners featuring clams and oysters were actually called "Feasts of the Shells." Clambakes became even more popular as the country looked to far history for a common national identity in the embers of the Civil War.

The picnic and clambake craze of the mid- to late 1800s was not just driven by nostalgia but also by industrialization that created wealth and leisure. The related expansion in transportation also made it easier for people with money and time to take shore vacations. (We are talking the era's upper-middle-class here versus the Astors, Duns, and Morgans who summered in mansion "cottages" at Newport and Narragansett.) At first, these clambakes consisted of small, informal groups of families and friends who would cook and

A cottage separates the eaters from the smoke and heat at this 1908 clambake at Wesquage Beach in Narragansett, Rhode Island.

eat shellfish that they gathered themselves. Then churches and men's clubs began to sponsor shore picnics. Some of those men's groups enjoyed their beachfront carousing so much that they built clubs for the express purpose of holding regular clambakes. Eventually, public clambake pavilions and shore dining halls accessible by train or steamboat sprung up on beachfront property all around Narragansett Bay and nearby waterfront Massachusetts. Ads of their destinations, schedules, and prices filled pages of local newspapers.

At its peak, in the late 1800s, three steamboat companies with multiple ships competed to bring passengers from Providence to more than 25 summer resorts and clubs on both sides of the Bay—a competition complicated by the companies' cross-ownership of their resort or hotel destinations.

As a result, according to one 1948 history, passengers who boarded a boat owned by the company that owned the Rocky Point resort "who held tickets for other resorts frequently found themselves carried to Rocky Point."

This same company fit "its wharf with heavy timbers topped with iron spikes and ran these timbers out when any opposing boat was seen approaching" Rocky Point. But instead of stopping or veering off, one competitive boat one day instead "passed the wharf at full speed . . . so closely that it struck the beams, sheering them off short." Rocky Point's "owners then built a high fence of wooden pickets at the end of the wharf"—which an opposition boat promptly demolished by ramming.

The steamboat lines were also behind many of the resort travel guides that were published at the time—hence the breathlessness of some of their descriptions: "The lovely Eden of our Bay," "a terrestrial Elysium," and "one of the most beautiful and romantic spots on the bay," were among the superlatives ascribed to Rocky Point, the latter by 1858's *A Guide to Providence*

Pleasure-seekers disembark from a steamboat at Rocky Point in this 1910 postcard.

Rocky Point Park as it appeared in a Continental Steamboat Company trade card in the late 1880s. The shore dinner hall is the long, low building on the water to the right.

River and Narragansett Bay from Providence to Newport, before it went on to describe "caves and subterranean passages of singular character . . ., its convenient sandy shore for bathing, and its extensive open-shaded saloons furnished with the various non-intoxicating refreshments."

The Past and the Present: Narragansett Sea and Shore, circa 1883, enthused over Rocky Point's "menagerie," including a bear who drank sarsaparilla from a bottle; "flying horses, where all juveniles must needs take a tilt; the bowling alley, where men try the scientific hand, and the summer theater, . . . with its bands of musicians and performers."

The same guide identified the Buttonwoods resort as the site of the "famous" and "toothsome" 1840 William Henry Harrison presidential campaign clambake and Field's Point as being "for the people of the city who wish to secure a shore dinner and a sniff of the sea breezes without having time to run far down the bay." (Dinner and a round-trip ride from Providence to this resort took only two hours and cost all of 70 cents.)

An ad for Warwick's Oakland Beach in another book boasted of free dancing "in a cool hall situated within a few feet of the bay" and its aquatic toboggan, "the first ever invented, consisting of boats sliding down a long inclined plane into the lake at lightning speed." Among the advertised attractions of the short-lived Vanity Fair: laughing galleries (?), infant incubators (??), "dazzling electrical illumination," airship and balloon ascensions, and a

Rocky Point Today

Rocky Point is still a park, albeit a lot less exciting one than many locals remember. The amusement park went bankrupt in 1996 and sat there rotting until nostalgic Rhode Islanders voted yes on a $10 million bond referendum to buy the property in 2010.

The park is largely undeveloped—parking is in a big dirt lot a long hike across a big expanse of grass to get to the water or anything else interesting. For the Rocky Point bereft, that means the rusting remnants of the Circle Swing and Skyliner rides and the peeling blue paint on cement marking the former site of "New England's Largest Salt Water Swimming Pool." There are interpretive plaques beside all the ruins and others that merely mark the spot of where something fun used to be. (There's also a decoy interpretive plaque by the park's compost toilet that defines TMI.)

The state has also rebuilt the pier where thousands of pleasure-seekers once disembarked from steamships and where moderns now fish for scup (a sign says you're limited to 30 a day of whatever-that-is). There are also hiking trails and swimming at a small urban beach.

Rocky Point fans in search of an interactive historic experience would be better off bringing in clam cakes and chowder from the Rocky Point Clam Shack and eating them at one of the picnic tables steps away from the site of the late "World's Largest Shore Dinner Hall."

Rocky Point State Park, 1 Rocky Point Ave., Warwick, RI, 401-884-2010, free, www.riparks.com.

---

building fire "show" called "Fighting the Flames" (the latter presumably not staged anywhere near the balloons).

Nevertheless, as *Picturesque Narragansett* put it in 1888: "The great moving cause impelling people to come [to all these places] is the famous Rhode Island clambake."

What exactly was the meal all these resort-goers were clam-oring for? Something a lot more than simply clams baked over a fire.

A traditional bake starts by digging a hole in the beach, then filling it with stones that are covered with wood that is set on fire. When the rocks are white-hot, seaweed, clams, fish, potatoes, onion, "green" (unhusked sweet) corn, and, sometimes, sausage and lobster are piled on in layers. Then the whole thing is covered by blankets or canvas and left to steam-cook until the clams pop open and everything else is infused with their flavor. Then the bake is "pulled" (i.e., unpacked and served), often alongside unbaked accompaniments such as chowder, beer, coffee, and watermelon.

As one 1882 guidebook published by the Continental Steamboat Company half-jokingly explained, "A clam dinner consists, first, of baked clams; second, of clam chowder; third, of baked clams; fourth, of fish chowder; fifth, of baked clams; sixth, of . . . fish; seventh, of baked clams" on up to the 25th

Clambake mainstays include lobster, clams, and corn.

course of baked clams. "If you wish any more clams. . . you are at liberty to speak to the waiter. No wonder everyone leaves . . . with a self-satisfied air, and walks to the boat with head erect. It is impossible . . . to stoop over."

Or, as Nettie in the 1800s New England-set musical *Carousel* sighs after polishing off her portion of a clambake and before bursting into the "A Real Nice Clambake" song: "Dunno as I shoulda et those last four dozen clams!"

The clambake was both an elaborate cooking ritual and a bacchanalian feast. But early 1800s ones did not include clam cakes.

Exactly when that very important ingredient—to the author of *The Great Clam Cake and Fritter Guide*, anyway—got added to the clambake menu is hard to say. A 1923 *Providence Journal* article titled "Resorts That Flourished When Dad Was a Boy" credits Field's Point, which was also among the first RI resorts to hold public clambakes. Field's Point bake master Russell Fenner's expanded bakes also included sweet potatoes, sliced onions, cucumbers, and Indian pudding. Fenner's successor, Colonel A. S. Atwell, added lobsters and soft-shell crabs. Fenner started work there in 1849, and Atwell started in 1888; so, if this 1923 article writer remembered what his dad said correctly, the clam cakes came in at Field's Point sometime before 1863 (when this same article says Silver Spring resort had them).

And he might not have: An 1858 *Providence Journal* brief about Ocean Cottage says it was then serving "as good a bake, as nice clam cakes and crisp fresh fish 'done to a turn,' as any other."

Workers tend the bake at Field's Point, the first or one of the first clubs to add clam cakes to the clambake menu.

Wherever and whenever clam cakes were first added, it's not hard to imagine why they were added: Bigger meals meant bigger revenues. At the Warwick men's club in 1909, members and guests could get a dinner for as little as $1 or as much as $5. "Could a man really pay $5 for a shore dinner?" an astonished *Providence Journal* reporter quizzed Warwick Club chef Otho Boon at the time. "That would include wines," Boon replied reassuringly. As well as littleneck clams, spaghetti, clam chowder, brown and white bread, fried eels, cucumber, lettuce, onion, radishes, clam bouillon, baked clams with melted butter, five kinds of potato, corn, bluefish, soft-shell crab, baked lobster, tomato and lettuce salad, frozen Tom and Jerrys, and clam cakes (or we wouldn't even be mentioning it).

At the Warwick Club, as elsewhere, these larger clambakes, or shore dinners, as they came to be called, were typically served in two sections, with games in-between. (These included baseball and potato sack, three-legged, and fat man races so appropriate to these eating orgies.) The first course—usually including the clam cakes—fueled the recreation and kept the edge off in the event the bake was running late.

But unfamiliarity with this dish bred contempt from a few vacationers who wrote about the dinners.

In 1893, a writer for the *Portland* (Maine) *Daily Express,* obviously more familiar with Maine's flat-style clam cakes, reported mainly enjoying his shoreline Massachusetts hotel clam dinner "except the clam fritters, . . . which seems an inflated doughnut. The other day a man who saw this kind of clam fritter for the first time thought it was a new kind of cottage pudding, and requested the waiter to take it back and suffuse it with hard sauce."

Clambake vs. Shore Dinner

In New England in the mid- to late 1800s, the terms clambake and shore dinners were thrown around frequently and, sometimes, interchangeably. But yes, there is a difference.

Clambakes are big gluttonous feasts cooked and served outdoors. The traditional early clambakes only included foods that were steamed as part of the bake (clams, corn on the cob, bluefish, potatoes, onion, sausage, brown bread, Indian pudding, etc.) or food and drink that didn't need baking (like pickles, watermelon, and beer).

Shore dinners were big gluttonous feasts served indoors (though usually in sight of water) and oftentimes cooked indoors, too. This allowed the menu to be expanded to include non-baked foods like chowder and clam cakes. They were part of the evolution of the Narragansett Bay eateries from primitive picnic spots to true shore resorts.

The few clambake menus that listed fried eel, clam chowder, and clam fritters on their menus near the beginning of the shore resort era are the exceptions that prove the rule.

Still, a simple meal of clam cakes and chowder does not and never has constituted a shore dinner. This is common sense to anyone who's lived in Rhode Island for more than five minutes, but it became the law of the land in 1949 when a clam cake concessionaire legally challenged Rocky Point Park's right to call clam cakes and chowder a shore dinner in an advertisement—which should give you an idea how strong feelings run about clammy things in Rhode Island.

In his ruling in favor of the plaintiff, Superior Court Judge Louis Cappelli stated that "any heretic choosing to tamper with the lineup of the sporting event known as the Rhode Island shore dinner must do so privately—preferably at night—in Massachusetts if possible."

Want a taste of this piece of Southern New England seafood history?

Aunt Carrie's, Iggy's, and Cap'n Jack's are among only a handful of Rhode Island restaurants that still serve shore dinners or simplified versions of the same (though no RI restaurateur, even today, would be stupid enough to use this term for a clam-cake-and-chowder combo).

Authentic outdoor clambakes are even rarer, reserved for extra-special private parties or occasional public events that book up way ahead. These include Kempenaar's Clambake Club in Middletown, Rhode Island (every July 3), the Acushnet (Massachusetts) Lions (in September), the town of Carver, Massachusetts (as part of Old Home Day every July), and the waterfront Castle Hill Inn in Newport, Rhode Island (two times every July).

Clam cakes were dessert at a rather taut shore dinner not enjoyed by Thomas Wentworth Higginson in August 1871 at a Rhode Island resort he did not name (to protect the guilty?). Higginson had the misfortune of being seated across from a talkative off-duty shore-dinner house waiter. "The baked clams is the only clean things to these dinners. You won't get a waiter to eat a shore dinner; they know too much. Have their own separate meal. Pie and tea," Higginson's dining companion told him.

Early in this piece for *Scribner's Monthly,* which was also reprinted in some newspapers, Higginson confesses to not liking clams—and Higginson is now infamous as the writer who told Emily Dickinson to forget trying to publish her poetry. So his parting feeling "that almost any other form of food would be [more] welcome" can probably be dismissed as the grumblings of a confirmed curmudgeon. Especially when compared to the following 1879 *Brooklyn Daily Eagle* report of clam cakes at a shore dinner at Pawtuxet:

"Only an epicurean's dream can picture the delights of those elegant, spontaneous clam cakes, of delicate, pungent aroma, browned, crisp and toothsome. . . . Even the natives, to the clam bake born, waxed enthusiastic; the Boston girl opposite, a novice like myself, was enraptured, and as for me, my sense of bliss rose to such a pitch that one more dish would have made me burst forth into poetic strains or . . . spontaneous dissolution. Fortunately for myself, or the party, the course finished with the clam cakes . . ."

If this is the voice of enthusiastic discovery, then Colonel Randall A. Harrington's was one of impartial experience when he called clam cakes the dish "without which a lot of folks would not enjoy a clam dinner." This was in 1907, when Harrington was managing both of Rhode Island's largest clam-cake-making parks.

Harrington's statement also just makes sense. Big and doughy, clam cakes render moot the Pilgrim's old complaint about fish's insubstantiality. Clams minced and hidden in fritters are also a lot more approachable and easier to eat than clams that are merely steamed or baked. In the local press, President Rutherford B. Hayes's June 1877 trip to Rocky Point was noted less for the first presidential phone call (to Alexander Graham Bell) than for his eating a baked clam with a fork instead of picking it up in his hands like "an honest" local "epicure."

Like many fried foods, especially ones associated with the shore and vacations, clam cakes are an indulgent treat, a savory counterpoint to the fair favorite mini doughnuts that predated fried clams by almost half a century. In fact, in Southern New

President Rutherford B. Hayes's baked clam misstep at Rocky Point made the front page of Frank Leslie's Illustrated Newspaper.

Excerpt from the New York Herald's Account of Horace Greeley's August 6, 1872, Attempt to Eat His Way into the White House Via a Rhode Island Clambake

"Rhode Island was in her glory today. A clambake at any time is one of the institutions upon which the little State prides herself; but to have one with 10,000 people and national flags and . . . an American brass band and Horace Greeley present was too much almost. . . . Such she had today at Silver Springs, a beautiful grove four miles down the bay. . . .

"By noon the grounds were thronged . . . with all kinds and classes of people from all parts of the country round. . . . Everything was Greeley on the grounds although the famous Philosopher had not yet arrived."

Little boys hawked "Greeley prize packages. Greeley . . . badges were sold at an enormous rate." And a picture dealer sold autographed *cartes-de-visite* of the Sage, the price rising from 20 cents to a half dollar before he was half sold out. "The lager beer saloons claimed a great portion of patronage" from the waiting crowds. . . . The appearance . . . was similar to . . . the . . . gardens of a German Schützenfest . . . except" for the "three huge green wood fires" that "glowed like smelting furnaces under cover of seaweed and tarpaulin in the process of baking about 10,000 clams."

At length, amid intense excitement, Horace arrived. "Hearty cheers went up from all lips. . . . The people crowded about . . . and shook hands violently with Mr. Greeley, cheering him and waving their hats and handkerchiefs without cessation, while the American brass band" . . . prophetically played "Hail to the Chief."

"The Clam-bake dinner was announced at 2 o'clock and" after meeting with local dignitaries, "Mr. Greeley . . . again breasted the beating 'surf' of humanity, and after desperate struggles, succeeded in reaching the dining hall." While waiting for service to begin, "crowds of ambitious individuals" who had "tried to scale the windows and steal their way into the honor of dining with a probable President . . . were . . . ignominiously expelled. . . . The clams were finally brought out piping hot, and the Philosopher, whose appetite had become clamorous, went to work upon the bivalves tooth and bait—that is, he used his singers and molars in accordance with the demand of stern necessity: for baked clams can't be eaten with a fork. The clam bake was not wholly, however a bake of clams. . . . There were clam chowder and clam cakes and fried clams in addition to the baked ones; . . . there were also baked potatoes and boiled corn."

Appetite satiated, the Philosopher "plunged once again into the raging sea" of bodies outside and resumed handshaking. A crowd of men was perched on a nearby fence to "look over the heads of the rest at . . . the genial face bobbing up and down under the too enthusiastic shakes of his admirers when suddenly the fence . . . gave way. Nobody was hurt in the fall, all 'the roosters'"—like the real feathered kind—"having succeeded in lighting on their feet on the right side.

"'That's typical, Mr. Greeley,' said a gentleman near the Sage. 'They were all on the fence but they tumbled over on your side.' Whereat the Philosopher [smiled]."

England, clam cakes are among the first in a long line of fried amusement park and boardwalk specialties that now extends to fried Mars Bars and Twinkie ridiculousness.

If clambakes and the clam cakes in them were mainly a wealthy or at least middle-class treat in the middle of the nineteenth century, it was everyman fare by its end. Labor laws passed to limit working hours of the immigrant factory workers who were fueling the region's boom-time economy gave them time to relax. And the new trolley lines gave them a way to get to the resorts, sometimes individually or with family, but also as part of large gatherings of unions, companies, and political groups.

The political gatherings could be particularly loud and raucous. Sent to New England in the 1880s to study oyster farms, Prussian professor Anton Siegafritz reported with alarm of "a sort of political assemblage called a clam bake, where speeches and music and songs are interspersed with profuse feasts upon a species of oyster called the clam. Vast crowds attend these celebrations, and no sooner are they gorged with the insidious comestible, than they become full of excitement and furores [sic]; swear themselves away in fealty to the most worthless demagogues; sing, fight, dance, gouge one another's eyes out and conduct themselves like madmen in a conflagration."

The *Providence Journal*'s repeated references to the calm that prevailed during presidential candidate William Henry Harrison's 1840 clambake at Buttonwoods is the exception that proves the rule. "As an illustration of the good order and decorum which prevailed we may mention that one entrance opened into a field of corn and none was trampled," the story concluded.

(See side story for a first-hand account of presidential candidate Horace Greeley's 1872 visit to Silver Springs.)

Whether for well or ill, these large political gatherings are credited with increasing the fame of the Rhode Island clambake and, by extension, the clam cake. By the late nineteenth century, recipes for clam cakes were in most East Coast-published cookbooks and newspaper women's sections.

This was also when business at the shore dinner resorts peaked—then dropped. Field's Point, for example, served 150,000 clambakes in 1907 but only 80,000 three years later, when it, not coincidentally, closed for good. By 1923, 10 other resorts had also gone out of business. The automobile killed off the

The Shore Glee

Clambakes that include alcohol could get rowdy, a benign symptom of this being off-key singing. Variations on "Yankee Doodle" were popular, especially at political gatherings. But the following "easy glee for the merry-hearted," offered by Frederic Denison in his 1883 tourist guide *The Past and the Present: Narragansett Sea and Shore*, is nonpartisan.

Let gouty monarchs share their shams
'Neath silken-wove pavilions
But give us Narragansett clams,
The banquet for the millions.
CHORUS
Yankee doodle, keep it up
Yankee doodle, dandy.
Mind the music and the step,
and with the girls be handy.
Along the Narragansett shore,
Polite in their salaams, sir,
Sat copper-colored kings of yore
And feasted on their clams, sir
REPEAT CHORUS
Successor to these doughty kings,
Sits now the Yankee nation,
And every jolly Yankee sings
His clam-orous collation.
REPEAT CHORUS
But how each valiant Yankee crams,
We surely need not tell, sir,
If only you bring on the clams
All smoking in the shell, sir.
FINAL CHORUS

steamboats, the trolleys, and many of the passenger train lines, as well as many of their resort destinations. And the 1938 hurricane leveled most of the rest.

Why didn't the clam cake die with them?

Because of Crescent Park and Rocky Point, archrival resorts on opposite sides of Narragansett Bay that survived and thrived by replacing the old-fashioned games that accompanied the traditional clambake experience in the early days with modern amusement park rides—thus keeping clam cakes and the rest of the shore dinner menu alive through the late twentieth century.

Captain William Winslow began ferrying church groups out to Rocky Point for picnics or clambakes on his good ship *Argo* in 1840. Rocky Point's

In the 1950s, Crescent Park offered this shore dinner extravaganza for only $4, including tax. Clam cakes are at the far left.

history and development tracked the shore resort industry in general except for longevity—Rocky Point didn't close until 1996.

Crescent Park opened as an amusement park on a crescent-shaped beach in 1886. By 1893, it was Rhode Island's second most popular resort. Famed carousel maker Charles Looff built several carousels for Crescent Park at the behest of park founder George Boyden, and Looff later became park manager and owner. Crescent Park closed in 1977.

Both places served all-you-can-eat shore dinners of nearly identical components in massive dining halls. But being larger, more popular, and longer-lasting, Rocky Point is the place most Rhode Islanders 40 and older think of when you say shore dinner or all-you-can-eat clam cakes.

"Mother" Winslow started providing food for the groups her steamboat captain husband brought to Rocky Point in 1859, and clam cakes were on that menu at least as early as 1878. By 1885, Rocky Point had a dinner hall big enough to serve a clambake to 1,000 people at a time.

"A thousand people . . . seated in rows on stools at long, uncovered, white-painted deal tables, and engaged in the discussion of a clam dinner . . .," opined one *Providence Journal* reporter in 1895. "The clamor of a thousand voices in unrestrained conversation, the rattle of tin and clatter of crockery and clam shells, the breeze blowing through the open sides of the pavilion, the playing of a brass band, maybe, the hailing and calling and rushing of waiters, the hammering of knives and forks on the table, and the ceaseless call for hot-clams, more hot-clams, chowder, baked-fish-here, melted butter, water-please, sweet-corn-this-way, brown-bread-right here, watermelon"; and, of course, clam cakes,

Crescent Park Today

Twenty-first-century habitués can get a taste of the fun of the old Crescent Park amusement park by taking a ride on one of the park's original carousels in its original location (directly across the street from the long-gone clam-cake-serving Shore Dinner Hall).

The Crescent Park Looff Carousel is not just any old carousel but instead one of the largest and most elaborate ever built by famed carousel maker Charles I. D. Looff.

Looff's carousel business was based in Brooklyn, New York, when he got the 1895 Crescent Park commission, but he moved his factory to the park in 1905. For the next five years, this carousel doubled as a showroom for prospective carousel buyers from around the country.

That's why its 61 horses, four chariots, and one camel span the carver's career and feature some of his finest work as well as the old brass-ring game—should any parents want to try to bring that old brass-ring "catch" phrase into the Generation Alpha's vocabulary.

Crescent Park Looff Carousel, open April to Labor Day, $2 per ride, 700 Bullocks Point Ave., Riverside, RI, 401-435-7518, www.crescentparkcarousel.org.

served with the baked fish to 250 people, while the other quarter sections of the hall chowed down on clams, chowder, or watermelon. Meanwhile, outside, hundreds more crowded the gate, waiting for the emptying of a section.

After eating his fill, the reporter strolled down toward the beach by an old shed with a slit running down its length through which quahog shells were flying "in a way at once mysterious and startling." He then finds inside, "three or four men opening quahogs for chowder." Later, in the kitchen, he observes clam cakes that "swim about and fry in a small pond of melted lard on top of a big oven. . . . Two hundred pounds of liquid lard bubbling and sizzling float the hundreds of cakes; one man drops in the dough from a huge tin dish full and a second is employed in turning and taking them out. Five barrels of flour per week represents the average consumption of clam cakes."

Now for the start of a 1975 *New York Times* story about this same place:

"It's a festive scene of medieval gluttony—3,900 men, women and children slurping, chomping, crunching, whacking open lobster claws, dipping steamed clams into drawn butter, shuttling ears of hot corn back and forth past clacking teeth and spitting out hundreds of thousands of watermelon seeds into their plates. . . . In a single day five tons of clam cakes, all shot out of a special cannon invented for the purpose and each deep-fried for seven minutes, will disappear down the gullets of these self-made eating champions in the world's largest shore dinner hall."

In 80 years, it seems like only the scale of the gluttony at Rocky Point changed.

In the 1970s through the 1990s, you didn't need to go on the park's Corkscrew or Flume rides for entertainment: You could just sit in your seat at the "World's Largest Shore Dinner Hall" and watch the college-kid waiters try to send a giant roll of white paper down one of the newly cleared 20-foot-long tables with just enough of a gentle push that it would stop at the end and not fall off. Diners would place bets on it.

There was also dramatics built into Rocky Point's all-you-can-eat menu options: Order only chowder-and-clam cakes with someone who got the shore dinner with lobster and you couldn't eat at the same table, newbies would realize with a shock after they'd already paid. This was so bargain-price chowder-and-clam cakes people couldn't sneak-eat lobster.

And people *were* always trying to test the limits of the bottomless plate policy.

Park president Conrad Ferla once expressed amazement about the Woonsocket man of French-Canadian descent who would show up every other week to down a gallon of chowder and two to three plates of clam cakes.

"You know those clam cakes are made with baking powder, baking soda—when you eat a lot of them and drink beer, you just swell up," he told a reporter with a head shake.

This from a guy who once drove a Harley into a park dining hall in full motorcycle gang regalia.

Also bringing clam cakes into the twentieth century were the roadside restaurants and drive-ins catering to the automobiles that killed off the old shore resorts. Places like Gus's, an Oakland Beach restaurant that served clam cakes whose doughboy annex later became Iggy's (p. 31). And Aunt Carrie's (p. 24) of Narragansett, an auto tourist camp and restaurant turned restaurant and takeout with an ice cream stand. Both date back to the 1920s, which was also, probably not coincidentally, when the commercial deep fryer came into its own, and both are now among the most popular places to get clam cakes in Rhode Island.

MEANWHILE IN MAINE . . .

There are parallels in the stories of clam cakes' rise to popularity in Rhode Island and Maine. In both places, clams were a plentiful resource in the early days, harvested and eaten by the local poor, then later also by wealthier visitors as recreational fare.

But the geography and timing were as different as Maine's clam cake patties are from Rhode Island's puff balls.

Once cars came in, clam cake stands sprouted up beside the water almost everywhere in Rhode Island. Whereas Maine's clam-cake culture is concentrated on the coast south of Portland. The recreational eating of clam cakes there accompanied the building of rail and trolley lines that brought tourists to the Scarborough-Saco area of Maine for the first time just as the big Rhode Island shore resorts that served clam cakes began their decline.

This was also about the time when commercial canneries sprung up along the Maine coast to capture and profit from excess seafood catch. The first clam cannery in the United States was built in 1878 at Pine Point in Scarborough, with clams sold under the Scarboro Beach name by Burnham & Morrill (a company now known mostly for their New England-style B&M baked beans). Today's best-selling brand of canned clams, Snow's, also got its start in Scarborough (in 1920). Food historian Sandra Oliver theorizes that clam cakes made with canned clams could have been a filling meal for families of modest means in these cannery towns. That was even true of families headed by clammers since they could sell fresh clams for more money. (And downeasters are famously frugal!)

But this is only a theory. Although Oliver lives in Maine and wrote *the* definitive history of New England seafoodery in *Saltwater Foodways*, she had to page through a copy of another book she wrote to confirm that it contained late local newspaper columnist Marjorie Standish's recipe for clam cakes.

"She lived in Machias, which suggests this dish was known further up the coast. But no, it's not like everyone here is going around saying, 'Let's make grandma's recipe for clam cakes today,'" Oliver says.

Brad Pollard, owner of the now-shuttered Cole Farms of Gray, Maine, a restaurant that was famed for its clam cakes, is down with Oliver's theory about the canning factories. "Chopped clams were cheap and readily available from places like Snow's," he says. Pollard further speculates that the clam cake "could have been an evolution of the clam casserole," another local dish made with chopped clam, egg, and crackers that was also "a quick, inexpensive way to feed your family."

Snow's canning factory in 1937

As for clam cakes' migration onto Maine restaurant menus: Many credit Harmon's, a brand of ready-made Maine-style clam cakes with roots in a Scarborough seafood restaurant that was famous for the dish in the 1940s and 1950s. (See p. 109 for more on Harmon's.)

But that idea is belied by the *Biddeford Weekly Journal*'s 1919 report of the Biddeford High School graduating class dinner at Tarbox's featuring lobster stew and clam cakes. And Ken Skilling was selling clam cakes at his Scarborough fried clam stand as early as 1934. (See p. 105 for more on his Ken's Place restaurant.)

Road food connoisseurs Jane and Michael Stern's description of their early 1990s clam cake experiences at Cole Farms and the Lobster Shack at Two Lights echoes the Biddeford High School class dinner. "In the vicinity of Portland on the coast of Maine, a favorite way with clams—especially as a side dish to a boiled lobster—is clam cakes," they wrote.

Snow's Sea Food Specials!

TO GIVE YOU A REAL NEW ENGLAND TREAT

MINCED CLAMS offer you a chance to prove your prowess as a housewife. Make clam stew, clam cocktail or clam chowder from it. 8½ oz. tin **32c**, 6 for **1.89**

CLAM CAKES prepared from clams, cracker meal, clam bouillon and seasoning. Make either six large or 12 small cakes. 8½ oz. **21c**, 6 for **1.23**

FISH CHOWDER in a concentrated new formula. Simply add a piece of butter and a pint of rich milk. Heat and serve . . . 15 oz. **27c**, 6 for **1.59**

CLAM CHOWDER in concentrated form. True N. E. style . . . fine ingredients. 15 oz. tin **27c**, 6 for **1.59**

LOBSTER NEWBURG containing tender lobster meat in a creamy sauce. Sherry-accented, ready to eat and serve on toast or in patties. The flavor is particularly subtle. 8½ oz. **53c**, 6 for **3.15**

Order by Mail or Phone HUBbard 2700 or ELIot 5000 'til 9 P. M.

JORDAN FOOD SHOP—THIRD FLOOR—ANNEX   D 159

Snow's late 1940s product lineup included already-made clam cakes in a can.

There, they went on to say, "Clam cakes are to lobster what hush puppies are to catfish throughout much of the South: a routine companion," though, even then, they noted how the clam cakes were starting to be replaced by a bag of potato chips at some places.

Today, Southeastern Maine restaurants more commonly sell clam cakes as an appetizer, in a bun like a hamburger or as part of a dinner plate with French fries, if they serve them at all.

Clams—even the ones without bellies—are no longer cheap enough for clam cakes to serve as a side-dish giveaway. And so, clam cake lovers are left with the few places near Scarborough that specialize in them (profiled on pp. 102–112).

Most other Maine clam shacks have either switched to making the similar but now better-known crab cakes or serve clam cakes by Harmon's, a storied local company that has twice in recent years been pulled back from the brink of extinction.

FROM NEW YORK TO NORTH CAROLINA

At the turn of the twentieth century, clam fritters appeared on the menus of big-city hotel restaurants and boardwalk joints up and down the Eastern seaboard. Hotels served them for breakfast as much, if not more, than for lunch or dinner. (And compared to New York's Hotel Champlain's other 1901 breakfast options of stewed kidneys or frizzled beef, clam fritters sound almost okay.)

And Nathan's hot dog scholar Lloyd Handwerker says it was the cheap and readily available clam—and not the hot dog—that first drew crowds to New York's Coney and City Islands in the late nineteenth and early twentieth centuries, including in its fritter and shore dinner presentations. But once the RI shore dinner craze was over and clams were no longer as cheap and plentiful, the clam fritters were gone.

That is except in Maine and Maryland and Virginia's Eastern Shore. Like chowder in New England, clam fritters on the coastal peninsular of Virginia started out as fishermen fare. In the days before outboard motors, clammers would work Hog Island Bay day and night for weeks at a time.

With limited space and no refrigeration, "if you caught fish or whatever, that's what you eat," waterman Kenny Marshall told Bernard Herman in Herman's *A South You Never Ate*. "You took lard and flour with you, that was the main two ingredients, and molasses. That was it. And salt and pepper"—i.e., exactly what you need to make clam fritters. And Marshall was only one of dozens of local residents who told Herman that they still make family recipes for clam fritters at home.

Herman's book credits the rural nature and geographic isolation of the Delmarva Peninsula for keeping this old food tradition alive. But clam fritters' popularity as the subject of fundraisers for area civic organizations, churches, and volunteer fire departments hints that these people are also now becoming too crunched for time to catch the clams and make their own fritters.

Most of these events are by and for locals. But because it's held in conjunction with their wildly popular pony crossings, the Chincoteague Volunteer Firemen's Carnival also draws tourists who are trying pancake-style clam fritters for the very first time.

For decades, the Chincoteague firemen shared the role of Eastern Shore clam-fritter evangelists with several women who ran restaurants and boarding houses on nearby Smith and Tangier Islands. Hilda Crockett of Chesapeake House on Tangier and Eloise Tyler of the Harbor Side Restaurant and Frances Kitching of the Frances Kitching Inn, both on Smith, became famous for clam fritters and other down-home local delicacies they fed visitors that ferries daily disgorged from the mainland. But only Kitching parlayed her grandmother's recipes and her fisherman husband's fresh catch into *New York Times* and *Washington Post* stories, private dinners for celebrities like Sylvester Stallone, and a cookbook that's still in print.

There, in a house only a clam shell's throw away from where Kitching was born, the famous and not-so sat on mismatched chairs at a long table groaning with platters of crab cakes, sliced ham, bean and macaroni salad, baked rockfish, hot baking powder biscuits, pickled carrots, crab loaf, clam chowder, fried apples, oyster puffs, crab soup, corn pudding and, of course, Eastern Shore-style clam fritters made with Bisquick and evaporated milk.

Frances Kitching

Kitching's cuisine was a curious amalgam of the island's fresh fish bounty and convenience products necessitated by an island's isolation transformed with the skill that "separates the professional from novice cooks," the *Washington Post's* Joan Nathan wrote of Kitching in 1981, six years before her boardinghouse-inn closed. A nephew quoted in Kitching's 2003 obituary said he was still fielding "five or six calls a day from all over the world asking if the inn is still open."

Mrs. Kitching's Clam Fritters

12 hard clams (large cherrystone size or manos), shucked with their juice

¼ teaspoon pepper

¼ cup evaporated milk

4 tablespoons self-rising flour or pancake or baking mix

1 egg

Corn or peanut oil for the grill

Place the clams and juice in a blender or food processor. Using a quick on-and-off method, blend clams until just minced. (They should not be pureed.)

Pour minced clams into a medium bowl; add pepper, milk, flour or baking mix, and egg and mix well.

Heat griddle or frying pan to about 375°F or medium-high, and grease lightly with oil. For each fritter, scoop out one teaspoonful of the mixture onto the hot frying pan. When just golden brown, turn with a spatula and lightly brown other side. Keep greasing frying pan as needed.

Yield: About 40 silver-dollar-sized fritters

From *Mrs. Kitching's Smith Island Cookbook*

And no history of clam fritters, including ones that are now mainly history, would be complete without a mention of Sea Breeze, North Carolina.

During its heyday from the 1930s to 1950s, this spit of land 12 miles south of Wilmington, North Carolina, was one of very few places where Black North Carolinians could go to enjoy the beach in peace, though not quiet. A Black-owned resort created for Blacks adjacent to the whites-only Carolina Beach, Sea Breeze had hotels, cottages, fishing piers, a bingo parlor, and an amusement park. But it was especially known for its "juke joints," halls where the dancing to the latest recordings and live bands earned Sea Breeze the nickname "Bop City," and its restaurants' clam fritters.

As described by Sadie Wade of Sadie's Place, a premiere fritter spot, to Sea Breeze scholar Jennifer J. Edwards in 1998, these fritters sound similar to the clam pancakes of Virginia's Eastern Shore except for the Sea Breeze version's finely chopped bell pepper and spices that Wade would not disclose.

Arthur Ross's Sea Breeze-Style Clam Fritters

Arthur Ross was probably the best-known Sea Breeze clam-fritter maker of the post-Bop City era. Though Ross never owned a restaurant, he made the fritters at community events, including the Sea Breeze Heritage Festival, the Pleasure Island Seafood, Blues and Jazz Festival, and Wilmington Riverfest. Ross died in 2021, but his adult children carry on his fritter-making legacy. Daughter Karen Colvin graciously agreed to share his recipe.

20 medium to large whole chowder clams, cleaned, shucked, and chopped, juice reserved and set aside

3 cups self-rising flour

½ large green pepper, chopped

1 large onion, chopped

2 large eggs, beaten

1 tablespoon Old Bay seasoning

1 tablespoon black pepper

1 teaspoon seasoning salt

1 tablespoon baking powder

Vegetable oil for frying

Combine clams and flour in a large bowl. Add all the other ingredients. Batter should have the consistency of pancake batter; if not, thin with reserved clam juice. Add a half-inch

Pancake-like Sea Breeze clam fritters

of oil to a cast iron skillet, and heat until very hot. Place batter in pan with a small spoon. Cook until fritter is brown on the bottom and bubbles appear on the top. Then flip and brown the other side. Serve hot with ketchup and hot sauce.

Yield: 20 to 25 fritters

How important were clam fritters in Sea Breeze? Important enough that the only play thus far written about this resort—*Summers at Seabreeze*, by Zach Hanner and performed at TheatreNOW in Wilmington in 2015—was in a dinner-theater format, so playgoers could eat fritters while the actors playing Sea Breeze restaurant owners argued over who made the best.

And re-creations of Sea Breeze fritters are, unfortunately, all people from away can get today. A triple threat of erosion-causing channel modifications, Hurricane Hazel (in 1954), and (ironically) Civil Rights legislation that opened up a whole country of other vacation destinations to Blacks, ultimately felled Sea Breeze.

But Sea Breeze-style fritters live on with the local families who still make them at home and in the memories of those old enough to remember when.

Chowder: A Clam Cake Lover's Guide

Chowder was part of the clambake menu expansion that also included clam cakes at Rhode Island resorts in the mid-1800s, although the two items weren't originally paired in any way or even necessarily served as part of the same course.

Today, in Rhode Island and nearby Massachusetts, the two dishes are considered as compatible and inseparable as peanut butter and jelly or hot dogs and beans. Although clam cakes and chowder are sold separately, they're also often available in discounted combo deals that alone can constitute a lunch or even dinner (for light eaters). Essentially, it's soup and bread. And it's the only way to order for confirmed clam cake dunkers.

As for the chowder: You choose by color from options that usually include white (aka New England), clear (aka Rhode Island), and/or red or some combination.

White is so ubiquitous as to hardly need an explanation. It contains milk or cream in addition to the usual clams, clam broth, and potatoes and is usually the only clam-chowder option in Maine and Massachusetts. And it's growing in popularity in Rhode Island, where it has even won some chowder contests. Taste-wise, cream is hard to beat.

But the clear chowder known as Rhode Island (though it can also be found on the eastern shore of Connecticut and the Outer Banks of North Carolina) is a better clam cake companion. Its austerity balances clam cakes' greasy fried indulgence. It's also closer to chowder's historic roots as a shipboard soup flavored with fish and thickened with cracker-like hardtack rather than milk or potatoes (both prone to spoilage). Contemporary versions of traditional Rhode Island clear clam chowder do contain potatoes and onion and little else to distract from the bracing briny broth of grayish hue that can take some getting used to. But as food historian Raymond Sokolov once said of clam chowder in general: "The plainness . . . is its hallmark and . . . genius."

Red is more complicated. Order this chowder at most Southern New England clam shacks that don't make their own chowder (which is most Southern New England clam shacks) and what you'll get is Manhattan clam chowder or what fans of Rhode Island-style chowder describe derisively as vegetable soup with clams.

The *Providence Journal*'s archives are brimming with outrage over tomato-containing clam chowder, like this 1947 letter by one Bivalve of Barrington:

"It has been blandly represented . . . on this page, under the privileges of free speech, that a Rhode Island clam chowder should have tomato. . . . If they want to call [this] a chowder, let them. . . . But let them not say it is a Rhode Island clam chowder. . . . Liberty is one thing, license another, and there are limits of social acceptability in every civilization."

Bivalve and his ilk are either not familiar with—or don't want to acknowledge—the tomato Rhode Island chowders served at Rocky

Squantum is the only mid-nineteenth-century Rhode Island club created to put on clambakes that is still at it.

Point, Crescent Park, and other Narragansett Bay clubs and resorts in the nineteenth and twentieth centuries.

Rocky Point's red chowder was particularly beloved and still is, judging from the number of Internet hits it gets, including one leading to Marilyn Bethune's multi-page paean on Roads&Kingdoms.

Rocky Point fan John Malone's memory of that chowder comes not from the Shore Dinner Hall but from two of the park's most stomach-churning rides.

"I will always remember the red chowder underneath the Spider and on the walls of the Tilt-A-Whirl," he told director David Bettencourt in the documentary *You Must Be This Tall: The Story of Rocky Point*.

East Providence's exclusive, 152-year-old Squantum Club also has a legendary red chowder that it still serves to members and at private, catered events. The recipe dates back to the late 1800s and is supposed to be top-secret, but it was printed in the Providence *Evening Bulletin* in 1913.

Rhode Island Clam Chowder

3 ounces salt pork or bacon, diced

1 large onion, finely chopped (equaling about 1 cup)

4 cups chopped clams

4 cups (32 ounces) bottled clam broth*

2 cups water

4 medium raw potatoes, preferably russet, diced (about 3 cups)

1 bay leaf

Salt and pepper to taste

Fry the salt pork or bacon in a large metal soup pot or flameproof casserole until crispy and brown. Add the onions and cook until translucent. Add the clams, clam broth, and water. Set over high heat and bring to a boil.

Add the potatoes and bay leaf and let the liquid return to a boil. Turn down the heat and simmer until the potatoes are tender but not falling apart (about 40 minutes). Remove bay leaf and serve.

Juice from fresh or canned clams can be substituted for any or all of the bottled kind

Yield: 6 servings

2
DELICIOUS DESTINATIONS

Southern New England is Mecca for clam cake lovers of the ball variety. The epicenter of Mecca is Rhode Island, especially the south coast and waterfront areas surrounding Narragansett Bay.

That's why in breaking down this part of New England by state, Rhode Island comes first. Stand order within states throughout this chapter is non-partisan alphabetical except for Aunt Carrie's and Iggy's (because fame and rivalry have their privileges).

Rhode Island clam-cake love is infectious and has spread to nearby Massachusetts and Connecticut. Do they know what they're doing? Sometimes. Is every Rhode Island clam cake maker great? Of course not. Like a really good clam-boat captain, this section will steer you away from troubled clam cake waters and in the right direction.

RHODE ISLAND–STYLE CLAM CAKES AND FRITTERS

RHODE ISLAND

AUNT CARRIE'S
1240 OCEAN RD., NARRAGANSETT, RI, 401-783-7930, AUNTCARRIESRI.COM

Who makes the best clam cakes? The majority of Rhode Islanders will answer this question, "Aunt Carrie's." Aunt Carrie's has won the annual Clamarati clam cake contest (see p. 126) so many times that it's been retired from the running. And it's one of only two Rhode Island restaurants to get an "America's Classics" award from the lah-de-dah James Beard Foundation.

It's not just because of Aunt Carrie's clam cakes, lobster BLTs, and cream pies. It's also because you get to eat this food in a cedar-shingled building air-conditioned only by ceiling fans and sea breezes coming off the marsh and through open windows—in other words, a place that has hardly changed since the screen doors first banged open and shut in 1925.

You may have heard that Aunt Carrie Cooper invented the clam cake. If you've read Chapter 1, you know that's not true. Rhode Islanders have been chowing down on clam cakes at no-frills bayside dining halls since the mid-1800s. But Aunt Carrie's is *the* place to have that old shore dinner hall experience today.

Aunt Carrie's founders, Carrie and Ulysses Cooper, with their daughter, Virginia (far left), in front of the restaurant in 1924

The restaurant has its roots in a snack stand Carrie Cooper and her lumber-dealer husband, Ulysses, set up by the Point Judith Lighthouse about a mile away from the current restaurant in 1920. Though she grew up in Southern Rhode Island, Carrie Campbell moved to Ulysses Cooper's Connecticut home when they married. But the couple returned to the Narragansett shore for camping vacations. At some point, Carrie decided to fry up fritters with the clams her kids dug out of the nearby mud flats, other campers picked up the delicious scent (and free handouts), and Ulysses saw a new business opportunity.

After five successful summers at the stand, the Coopers bought a piece of nearby land to build a restaurant with indoor dining. Eventually, they added a gas station and a tourist campground frequented by paying guests but also Carrie's siblings and their kids. Hence the name Aunt Carrie's.

The Coopers' daughter Gertrude and her husband, William Foy, took over from her parents in 1953, and their son, Bill, and his wife, Elsie, in turn, in 1984. Bill and Elsie met working at Aunt Carrie's as teenagers—he was in the kitchen making clam cakes, and she was at the takeout counter, delivering lots of meaningful glances with her orders.

Says Foy, "When he proposed, I told him, 'Only if I have nothing to do with the restaurant.' I did not want to be there all the time the way my mother-in-law was." Decades later, there is still a hint of resentment when she recalls having to get married on a Tuesday—the day the restaurant has always been closed—so her in-laws could attend.

But she eventually did return to working at Aunt Carrie's—at first, when she was laid off from a computer programming job; later, when Gertrude had eye surgery—in the process discovering that she was good at the books and enjoyed interacting with customers.

Talking with her young staff and a reporter, she is reserved but friendly; responsive but no-nonsense—the kind of boss who once fired her own daughter. "She wasn't doing the work," she says with a shrug and a smirk.

When her husband died in 1994, it fell to Foy to keep his family's now century-old business alive and thriving. Despite her early misgivings, it's a role she has embraced.

"I'm very, very careful with changes," she says, in most decisions leaning heavily on the side of "keeping it the way it was," from the lace curtains and yellow-and-green paint scheme to the food.

"We've never done mozzarella sticks, even when it was all the rage," she says proudly. "And we still offer complete dinners as well as a la carte. You won't see that very many places these days." In fact, she continues, "If you look at our menu today and the ones from the 1950s, you won't see a whole lot of difference."

At the top of all Aunt Carrie's menus, past and present, are the best-selling clam cakes. The secret to their popularity? The beef lard they're cooked in here and few other places. Modern health concerns with that old-fashioned fat have scared other restaurants away and even makes Foy reluctant to talk about it (until she was reminded that their secret ingredient was outed during their 2012 appearance on *Diners, Drive-Ins and Dives*).

Lard "gives the clam cakes flavor," she says, especially if it's not changed too often. "If the oil is too old, the clam cakes can get too dark. But if it's *too* clean, the cakes won't taste like anything." She puts the sweet spot at two days.

One recent summer weekday, teen clam cake maker Maddox Lima dumped a quart of broken eggs, two gallons of shucked sea clams, and four big scoops of seasoned flour in a huge metal pot and began stirring with a five-pound, long-handled paddle. Making batter in this quantity and way is a surprisingly physical job that Foy says, "I'm not strong enough for anymore." After emptying a fifth of the batter into a smaller, long-handled pot, Lima dips an old silver serving spoon in and drops a baseball-sized clump into one of two bubbling fryolators, over and over and over. The imprecision of that antique tool (versus the ice cream scoops most places use) explains why Aunt Carrie's clam cakes have so many crusty appendages. (One past Aunt Carrie's kitchen crew created a zoo from clam cakes resembling animals.)

Once the fryer is full of dancing dough balls, Lima lowers a screen that keeps them submerged in the fat. After they brown up, he sticks a fork in one to check for doneness before fishing them out with a wire-mesh strainer.

At peak summertime, when customers order up to 2,000 clam cakes a day, Lima's job will be split among three people: one making the batter, one dropping and cooking, and the final bagging and plating the finished cakes.

The clam cakes are available as a stand-alone snack or appetizer, with one of three chowders (a Rhode Island-style clear, and red and white ones based on it) or as the opening salvo of a marathon, old-fashioned shore dinner that also includes steamed clams, fish and chips (featuring local flounder), a pound-and-a-half Point Judith lobster, and your choice of a homemade dessert.

Oh, those desserts! Pies date back to the 1920s and include a seasonal rhubarb, multiple cream pies, the non-traditional key lime, and Foy's personal favorite, apple; all are famed for their flaky and flavorful crusts. Here again, the secret is solid fat, and this time, it's the vegetable kind. Their cinnamon-raisin bread is so popular that it's now the sole occupant of their bread baskets. "Nobody ate the white," Foy notes, though it's also homemade. Between all that and the seasonal biscuit-style strawberry shortcake and

Elsie Foy (center), Phillip and Laura Perron, and daughters Willow (left) and Ember, representing the third, fourth, and, potentially, fifth generation of family ownership of Aunt Carrie's.

old-fashioned Indian pudding (see side story), let's just say it's good that the antique scale in Aunt Carrie's dining room is not working.

Foy's elder daughter, Amy, survived her early firing to become the maker of all these delicious endings. Her younger daughter, Laura, started doing payroll when she had her first baby and, in a process that echoes Foy's own gradual easing into the business, now shares managing duties with husband Phillip Perron. The restaurant's most successful new item, a lobster BLT, was Perron's idea. But his attempts to modernize the menu with dishes featuring the nationally popular shrimp and salmon—which Foy calls "not Rhode Island food"—have not worked out as well.

"People are not coming to Aunt Carrie's for baked stuffed shrimp: They're coming here to get what they've always gotten," she says firmly.

They're also there to talk to Foy, the Aunt Carrie of her day.

"People tell me how their parents brought them here when they were kids or about coming here on their first date." Sometimes they just want to say hello or goodbye. For this reason, Foy says, "I can't have a job in the kitchen the first and last weekends of the season."

Ever True to Aunt Carrie's U

You know a place is an institution when it has its own alumni association.

Although not a formal thing, Aunt Carrie's owner Elsie Foy says she knows of at least three groups of former Aunt Carrie's workers who get together regularly, including eight waitresses from the 1970s who meet monthly, 1990s staff who gather once or twice a year, and a group of Carrie's alums in their 30s who live locally and see each other frequently.

This is not to mention multiple summer romances that turned into marriages or generations of families who have worked there forming "alumni groups" who see one another daily.

These close relationships were forged not just in the heat of Aunt Carrie's kitchen but also at the beach on Tuesdays, when the restaurant was closed, or at a long-running, annual, end-of-season party, where staff received joke prizes, like the bulldozer award for the pushiest waitress, as former waitress Heidi Lessard once recalled.

Aunt Carrie's alums can be likened to combat buddies in having lifelong ties formed while working very intensely together at an impressionable time.

Indian Pudding
(Because the Name Corn Pudding Was Already Taken)

Indian pudding is called that because it was first made by Indigenous peoples.

Like the also seemingly self-evident "The most qualified person always gets the job," this is disappointingly not true.

But Indian pudding *is* one of America's oldest desserts, the colonists' adaptation of the puddings they loved back in England to include the cornmeal that was readily available and popular with their Native neighbors in the New World.

In fact, the colonists' association of corn and Native Americans was so strong that they used the words corn and Indian almost interchangeably: hence, the Indian pudding name. There are not one or two but three recipes for it in *American Cookery* by Amelia Simmons, America's first cookbook.

Common Accompaniments to Clam Cakes/Fritters in Southern New England

(listed in order of acceptability/popularity)

Nothing, salt, chowder, tartar sauce, hot sauce, and, rarely, malt vinegar. "We can always tell when we've got a tourist at the counter because they ask for honey or maple syrup," says Elsie Foy of Aunt Carrie's.

What's it like? Elsie Foy instructs her young servers at Aunt Carrie's—one of few restaurants to still feature the dish—to answer that question with the question: "Do you like gingerbread?" And most recipes for Indian pudding do feature a bracing blast of old-fashioned ginger and molasses flavors as well as corn.

But the texture (smooth) and the temperature (warm) make the past go down easy—especially when the strong flavors are mitigated with the traditional vanilla ice cream or whipped cream.

Indian Pudding Something Like Aunt Carrie's

New Englanders used to cook their Indian pudding in brick ovens with their baked beans: hence the low temperature and (by modern cooking standards) long cooking time.

   3 cups whole milk, divided

   ½ cup cornmeal

   ⅛ teaspoon salt

   ⅛ teaspoon baking soda

   2 tablespoons butter, melted

   1 egg, beaten

   ¼ cup molasses

   2 tablespoons dark brown sugar

   ½ teaspoon cinnamon

   ¼ teaspoon ginger

Grease a 2-quart casserole dish. Preheat oven to 325°F. In a large saucepan, combine 2 cups of the milk with the cornmeal, salt, baking soda, and butter. Cook over medium-high heat, constantly stirring until the mixture thickens to the texture of polenta (at least 5 minutes).

In a small bowl, combine egg, molasses, brown sugar, cinnamon, ginger, and the remaining cup of milk until well-blended. Stir into cornmeal mixture. Pour into casserole dish, then set into a larger dish filled with water and bake uncovered for 1 ½ to 2 hours (adding more water to the larger pan if too much evaporates). Pudding should be softly firm, and a knife inserted in the center should come out clean. Serve warm with vanilla ice cream or whipped cream.

Yield: 4 to 6 servings

Aunt Carrie's V. Iggy's

After 80 years of being *the* clam cake queen of Point Judith, Aunt Carrie's couldn't have been happy to see an Iggy's stand open right across the street.

But the move was a boon for clam-cake fans who want to experience the two most famous names in clam cakes in Rhode Island in one place—and since Iggy's 2015 move to a new building 300 feet up the street, work off a few of those newly acquired calories trudging between.

And, indeed, Aunt Carrie's owner Elsie Foy says it's not uncommon for her to overhear people who are sitting in lawn chairs outside her office discussing the pros and cons of chowders and clam cakes they have taken out from both restaurants.

The Envelope Please

This book is not a contest. Still, a lifetime of eating Southern New England clam cakes and fritters, including recent tastings at more than 30 area restaurants and stands, has given me an opinion about what makes a great ball-style clam cake.

First and most important, it must arrive at your table or the pickup window hot from the fryer.

The crust must be crunchy and golden in color, rather than brown like that Providence university or the women who spend the entire summer lying on Scarborough Beach.

The inside should be light and airy rather than gluey, greasy, or rubbery (i.e., after eating one, your jaw should not ache). Placing a bag of them on your car's floor should not require a visit from an oil spill remediation team. Each clam cake individually should not resemble a lethal projectile or, once consumed, sink to the bottom of your stomach like a rock.

The cake should taste of clam, like something from the sea, or, at minimum, like something good. Containing visible bits of actual clam is optional but will get you extra points. So will making this clam cake from your own recipe, so that your clam cake is not good in the exact same way as everyone else's. (Boring!)

Of course, this is the Platonic ideal of a clam cake. Among the many other factors that can come into play when picking favorites are the atmosphere, history, and *je ne sais quoi* of the clam-cake-making place and your own history with it. That is to say, if after your childhood trips to the beach, your family always went to George's, George's will likely always and forever make your favorite clam cakes—and you will not hear an argument from me on that.

The above basic requirements having been met, the experience of eating a clam cake should ideally begin with a big crunch, continue with dough that almost melts in your mouth, and end with the satisfying chewing of slightly tough clam. (Chewing on anything before or besides the clam is a problem, Houston.)

Desserts aside (Iggy's has the doughboys; Aunt Carrie's has pies and ice cream), the two restaurants' menus are quite similar. Invited to explain the difference between his clam cakes and Aunt Carrie's, Iggy's owner David Gravino says only, "Ours are smaller and rounder"—hardly enough jet fuel to propel most people from one place or the other. A strong preference is typically motivated by habit, family tradition, or their totally different atmospheres: Aunt Carrie's full-service, sea-breeze-cooled wooden mess hall is like eating back in time; Iggy's Narragansett's New England McMansion is a totally of-this-moment takeout with digital signs, online ordering and delivery, and buzz-building long lines.

IGGY'S DOUGHBOYS AND CHOWDER HOUSE
889 OAKLAND BEACH AVE., WARWICK, RI, 401-737-9459, AND
1151 POINT JUDITH RD., NARRAGANSETT, RI, 401-783-5608,
IGGYSRI.COM

Twenty years ago, Iggy's was just another neighborhood clam cake shack, known by locals but top-of-mind for few others, its blue-collar Oakland Beach home being well past its prime.

Today, Iggy's is the second biggest name in clam cakes after stalwart Aunt Carrie's and is the RI clam-cake restaurant most likely to become a national chain.

What's behind Iggy's doughboy-like rise? It's actually a who: David Gravino, son of Iggy's late founder Gaetano "Iggy" Gravino, and a "huge fan of Disney" who has, in fact, transformed his dad's old

Iggy's owner David Gravino shows how it's done.

snack shack into the beginnings of a fried-food kingdom.

The story of this transformation begins with a dramatic deathbed promise. Iggy Gravino was a hairdresser who took over a concession stand known as Mrs. Gus's Doughboys in 1989 as a side, summer-only business. But, his son says, "He enjoyed doing it. He loved making the dough and chatting with people"—loved it so much, in fact, that it was his dying wish that the business stay in the family.

At the time, David was a senior at Johnson & Wales University with an eye to a career at a big hotel chain. But he set that aside to honor "his father's wish, and, in doing so, had a vision," as Iggy's website's About Us page inspiringly explains.

Seeing beyond the tiny shack with the even tinier menu and a beach "that had fallen into disrepair," the website copy continues, David saw the Oakland

Beach of its 1930s amusement park heyday "married with the Oakland Beach of the future."

Or, as David himself explains, a lot less loftily, "I could see it as year-round business."

Within three years of his father's 1994 death, David realized his vision by adding an indoor dining room and a lot more items to the menu. Three years after that, he opened a seasonal Iggy's across the street from Aunt Carrie's in Narragansett, placing himself in head-to-head competition with the most famous and beloved clam cake maker in Southern New England.

Still, Gravino wasn't done. In 2015, he upgraded again with a new ice cream stand and higher-end, full-service Boardwalk restaurant in Oakland Beach, as well as a grand new building in the Cape Cod-style in Narragansett.

Speaking from his equally modern and spiffy seaside cottage office adjacent to his Warwick restaurant complex (a stark contrast to the storage room corner most clam shack owners use), Gravino estimates Iggy's current business at 30 times what it was when his father ran it and says he sells up to 1,000 dozen clam cakes and 400 gallons of chowder daily between his two locations in the peak summer season.

Visits to both locations provide proof. The size and signage at the parking area in Warwick screams major tourist attraction. The perpetual traffic jam on the one-way street you must go down to get to Iggy's (and the public beach) just adds to the excitement. Iggy's Oakland Beach is not so much an eatery as a collection of eating experiences that includes a takeout clam shack, ice cream stand, full-service restaurant, picnic spot, and gazebo bar, all steps from the water.

The 15 people waiting for orders on the big wrap-around porch of Iggy's Narragansett on another July afternoon was only small compared to the

Iggy Narragansett's garden-like seating area

number waiting to order: That line went down the steps and stretched along the sidewalk. Unlike competitor Aunt Carrie's, Iggy's Narragansett has no salt marsh or waitress service but instead modern restaurant amenities like digital menu boards and online ordering, and a semi-hidden garden picnic area clearly preferred by many. (See p. 30 for more on Aunt Carrie's V. Iggy's.)

Iggy's visibility has also been raised by appearances on CBS's *Early Show* (praising their chowder) and the 2020 Democratic National Convention (see side story), and their collaboration with online food marketplace Goldbelly. Although most makers say clam cakes cannot be frozen and reheated to anywhere near just-fried deliciousness, up to 100 clam cake land ex-pats shell out $60 to Iggy's on Goldbelly daily in hopes that they can.

Clam cakes served up hot at the stands are light in color, uniformly shaped, and so large that the dough dominates. Iggy's three clam chowders are three separate recipes and not—as elsewhere—cream or tomatoes added to clear. Gravino seems especially proud of the red, a complex creation from his mom, Sally.

Gravino says that clam cakes and chowder alone account for about 60 percent of Iggy's business.

Unique to Iggy's is the doughboy—you won't find it on any other well-known local clam cake restaurant menu.

Doughboys are another name for the fried dough that's long been sold at amusement parks and fairs throughout New England and are a vestige of Iggy's Oakland Beach park past. Although fried dough can be savory and served with tomato sauce, doughboys are always sweet and covered in powdered, granulated, or cinnamon sugar and resemble a raised doughnut.

Doughboys are another thing shaped by David's vision. Although traditionally sold by the half or whole dozen bag and vigorously shaken to maximize the amount of sugar adhering to the hot dough, Gravino told *Rhode Island Monthly* magazine in 2015 that "I always knew I wanted to . . . incorporate doughboys into a sundae."

Hence Iggy's Colossal (with eight scoops of ice cream, four doughboys, and four toppings) and comparatively dainty regular doughboy sundaes (with just three scoops of ice cream and two doughboys).

Thanks to David's dreaming, you can also get doughboys in a shake, cut up into an ice cream topping, and (at the Boardwalk sit-down restaurant) in a basket with three dipping sauces.

"I nailed doughboys for all kinds of eaters," Gravino immodestly proclaims. Either that or he has made them nearly impossible to escape at Iggy's: It depends on how you feel about doughboys.

What's next for Iggy's? Food trucks and, eventually, franchising at seaside resorts across the country.

"Maine lobster rolls and New England clam chowder are now sold in every state in the country. Why not clam cakes?" Gravino wonders.

➤➤ If the line is too long at Iggy's, you might want to drive the 6 miles around Greenwich Bay to this classy waterfront **Chelo's Hometown Bar and Grille** (1 Masthead Dr., Warwick, RI, 401-884-3000, chelos.com). The family restaurant chain started in the French-Canadian-populated northern part of Rhode Island in 1955 with an ultra-crispy battered fish-and-chip dish for which it is still famed. The clam cakes followed sometime after, and together with their creamy New England-style chowder, make up the three best-selling dishes at this seasonal Warwick location—not surprising, given its marina setting. The good news is you can get clam cakes made with Chelo's same proprietary clam cake mix as well as their fish and chips, French-Canadian pork pie, roast beef sandwiches, and homemade cream pies year-round at any one of the other seven Chelo's around the state.

This makes Chelo's not just the only chain restaurant in Southern New England with clam cakes but also the majority restaurant supplier of clam cakes in the region in the off-season.

King Calamari

Clam cakes are the most popular seafood appetizer at restaurants in Rhode Island by far. And yet calamari is Rhode Island's official state appetizer.

How can that be? As with most other puzzles in the public arena, money and politics are involved.

Though clams are the foundation of some of the state's most popular and unique dinner openers—i.e., clam cakes, clam chowder, and stuffed clams—that shellfish is no longer as plentiful in local waters. Squid is now the biggest seafood business in Rhode Island, an $18-million-dollar industry accounting for more than half of all the calamari-to-be caught in the Northeast.

And that's why RI Representative/Democratic Party Chair Joseph M. McNamara picked a time when his state was making headlines for one of the highest unemployment rates in the nation to introduce legislation to crown calamari Rhode Island's appetizer king. "I'm tired of hearing the naysayers and Doctor Dooms that are really putting down our state. It's time we step forward and celebrate our successes," he explained in 2013.

What ensued was one of the Rhode Island legislature's more contentious battles. At a hearing fueled by calamari dish samples (though McNamara denied any "squid pro quo"), legislators debated the merits of seafood dishes like Elite Yelpers. "Why have a dish that is done everywhere in the US be the state appetizer?" asked chef Ben Sukle in one of many local newspaper stories on the proposed legislation. Why not something unique to Rhode Island?—like clam cakes, I would suggest.

Many lamented the waste of legislative time and money, not to mention "what idiots we look like . . . holding public hearings and cooking demonstrations at the State House while seven communities in the state face bankruptcy," wrote *Woonsocket Call* columnist Roger Bouchard.

When the bill failed, McNamara decried both petty politics and the leg-islator who "used symbols out of *Godfather I* and left the dead squid on the desk to send a message." But when he reintroduced the bill the next year as a way to educate the legends of squid squeamish, it passed.

And McNamara's squid boosterism continues, judging by his appearance on the roll call vote that was the comic hit of the 2020 Democratic National Convention.

While other states used their video clip moment during the largely virtual convention to tout local landmarks or address social issues, McNamara stood on a beach and hawked "our state appetizer, calamari . . . available directly from the fisherman in all 50 states," a masked chef by his side silently holding a platter of the breaded fried rings with cherry peppers.

Called everything from "ninja chef" to Roger Williams on social media ("A rare photo of Roger Williams and his calamari founding the colony of Rhode Island," tweeted *Time* correspondent Charlotte Alter), this guy was actually John Bordieri, executive chef at Iggy's Boardwalk in Warwick. And between its Warwick and Narragansett locations, Iggy's sells between 300 and 500 pounds of fried calamari appetizers per week in the summer.

But their clam cakes sell even better.

Rhode Island-Style Calamari

As some RI calamari-bill detractors pointed out, calamari are an appetizer at restaurants anyplace that has a significant Italian population. Typically, the rings are simply breaded and fried. Rhode Islanders usually up the indul-gence by finishing the dish with oil or butter, garlic, and banana peppers as in this recipe courtesy of the DNC roll-call-famous Iggy's.

½ cup flour

½ cup cornmeal

¼ cup cornstarch

1 teaspoon garlic powder

2 teaspoon salt

1 teaspoon pepper

1 pound cleaned squid calamari, tubes cut into rings and tentacles left whole

2 eggs lightly beaten

Vegetable oil for frying

4 tablespoons butter

1 cup sliced banana peppers, mix of red and green

Lemon wedges

Fresh parsley chopped for garnish

In a medium bowl, whisk together flour, cornmeal, cornstarch, garlic powder, salt, and pepper. Dip calamari in egg, then in flour mixture. Place on a plate as you go.

Heat a Dutch oven on medium heat with oil, about 2 inches high, until it reaches 375°F.

Fry calamari in batches until browned, about 1 to 2 minutes each side. Remove from oil and set aside.

In a separate large pan, melt butter over medium heat. Sauté the peppers until tender. Add the calamari and toss to coat. Serve with lemon wedges and top with parsley.

Yield: 4 servings

AMARAL'S FISH & CHIPS
4 REDMOND ST., WARREN, RI, 401-247-0675,
AMARALSFISHANDCHIPS.COM

Amaral's is the *Cheers* of Rhode Island clam cake sellers—for all those who missed that 1980s TV bar comedy, meaning a place where everybody knows everybody.

Sit in this little box of a building on the industrial side of waterfront Warren less than a mile from Blount Clam Shack (see p. 41) but in another universe in atmosphere and feel—and you will witness more (and more friendly) personal interactions than at the typical family dinner.

"How's Josh?" one young takeout customer asked owner Donald Amaral of Don's son one recent Tuesday lunchtime, before explaining that he knew Josh from a long-ago karate class.

A few minutes later, Don's nephew, Brian, stopped on his way back to the kitchen from delivering an order to ask another customer how his new car was working out.

And when someone questions his bill, Don studies it. "Just trying to see how much you'd be willing to pay," he says with a chuckle while making the adjustment.

Amaral's was originally Rego's. Don and his brother, Tony, bought the fish and chippery from Tony's former boss, Manny Rego, in 1984, and they still use some of Rego's recipes.

The English batter-style fish and chips have made several "best of" lists (these awards are framed and displayed on one wall) and account for about half of all store sales. Asked why they didn't cut up and sell the giant fish that is mounted on the entrance to the kitchen, Don says, "Because we use haddock for our fish and chips and that's striper."

The crispy, not-too-heavy clam cakes are made in their own fryer with Drum Rock batter that is mixed up throughout the day. "Otherwise, it gets stale," Don explains with just a hint of a Portuguese accent.

The Amarals also expanded the menu to include family Portuguese favorites like blade meat grinders (translation: marinated pork sub sandwiches), kale soup, and sweet bread (Wednesdays through Fridays). For years, the bread was made by Don and Tony's mother, Zelia, but since her 2019 passing, it has been made by her grandson Brian.

Brian, Don, and Tony keep the place humming most days, but if you want to meet even more Amarals, visit on Fridays, when they do more business than all the other days combined, and Don's sons and sisters often stop by to help out.

They also sell fried smelts (one two-year-old regular snacks on them like French fries, Don notes with a smile) and Willow Tree sandwiches. The Amarals used to make their own chicken salad but relented to popular demand for this storied local brand. (See p. 102 for more on Willow Tree.) It is among very few menu items not made on-premises.

Amaral's opens at 9 a.m.—not to sell fried seafood—but instead to fulfill its role as the unofficial town senior center.

"Quite a few retired gentlemen come in here in the morning to drink coffee and solve the world's problems," Don says.

THE RIGHT STUFFIES

Pop quiz. A stuffie is:

a) A child's plaything

b) "Clam meatloaf in an ashtray," in the words of Rhode Island songwriter Jon Campbell (see p. 124)

c) One-third of the holy trinity of Southern New England clam cuisine that also includes clam chowder and clam cakes

The answer is: d) All of the above, although, for the purposes of this book, we'll stick with the seafood meanings.

And like chowder and clam cakes, stuffies, or stuffed quahogs, are a product of Yankee thrift: They're yet another use for the big, tough quahog clam;

in this case, in combination with the even less valuable stale bread. Stuffies are usually served as an appetizer with the sometimes-hidden goal of filling people up before more expensive menu items like lobster and scallops.

Though that's not actually the reason they're called stuffies. It's really because of the way a stuffing-like mixture of celery, onion, garlic, bread or cracker crumbs, and chopped quahog clams (and sometimes also hot sauce, bacon, or spicy sausage like Portuguese chourico) are "stuffed" into the empty quahog shells now transformed into baking vessels, then into eating dishes with built-in certificates of freshness and authenticity.

Except when they aren't fresh and authentic. Although stuffies are served virtually every place that serves clam cakes and chowder, they aren't all made in-house. Unlike clam cakes, stuffies can be purchased premade and frozen and even (horror of horrors) packed in faux (plastic) clam shells.

To save yourself from that fate, get them at Amaral's or make your own from the following recipe.

RI Stuffies

12 quahogs in the shell

4 tablespoons (½ stick) unsalted butter

½ cup onion, finely chopped

1 tablespoon garlic, minced

¼ cup bell pepper or celery or some combination, finely chopped (optional)

½ pound ground chourico (or other spicy sausages)

1 cup fresh bread crumbs (from several slices of bread)

½ teaspoon paprika

Preheat oven to 350°F. Rinse and scrub quahogs, then steam them in a covered pan with 2 inches of water until they open. Shuck the clams, separating and cleaning the shell halves after adding their juice to the clam water. Strain this clam liquid through cheesecloth to remove any sand. Finely chop the quahog meat by hand or in a food processor. Melt butter in a large saucepan. Add onion and garlic and bell pepper and celery (if using) and chourico and sauté until meat is browned and the vegetables are limp.

Combine onion/sausage mixture in a large bowl with the chopped quahogs, bread crumbs, and paprika and add strained quahog water until the mixture is moist. Place 12 to 16 of the quahog shell halves on a cookie sheet and mound each with the mixture. Bake 20 minutes, or until edges of filling are crisp. Serve with lemon wedges and hot sauce.

Yield: 12 to 16 stuffies

ANTHONY'S SEAFOOD
963 AQUIDNECK BLVD., MIDDLETOWN, RI, 401-846-9620,
ANTHONYSSEAFOOD.NET

If Monahan's and Evelyn's are among the prettiest places to eat a clam cake, Anthony's is one of the most mundane. This former truck-repair facility sits between a gym and an office building at the back of a long, narrow parking lot on busy Route 138.

Go left upon entering and you'll enter a gleaming seafood market; turn right and you'll see the ordering counter, 1970s-era wood-and-tan-upholstered booths, and enclosed porch that is Anthony's restaurant. In warm weather, there's also the option to sit on old lobster-packing boxes at an outdoor patio in sight of the cars and the lines. And yes, in the summer, there will be some.

It must be the food: simple but satisfying clam cakes, best-selling breaded fish and chips, and beloved Portuguese fish chowder, as well as the Kung Pao calamari celebrated in a 2012 episode of *Diners, Drive-Ins and Dives.*

Anthony's has deep roots in the Newport fishing industry. Among the anchors and buoys decorating the walls of the indoor patio are paintings of two fishing vessels named for the grandparents of current owners Stephen and Michael Bucolo. Grandfather Mariano Bucolo was a partner in a Newport wholesale fish market, but it was his son, restaurant namesake Anthony, who started selling the family catch to the public, first from a market, and later at a floating restaurant in an old boat.

"As kids we'd spend 10 to 12 hours a day unloading the fish, nailing the corners on the wooden boxes of ice and fish, which is kind of telling you my age," Stephen admits. Stephen was 19 and splitting his time between classes at Johnson & Wales and bartending at the restaurant when the manager quit, and his father asked if he could fill in temporarily. "I never looked back," Stephen says.

Stephen was in the middle of another 12-hour shift the late fall day I stopped by. This time the cause was his chef's emergency heart surgery, but Anthony's was also otherwise short-staffed and facing rising prices that were exacerbating their struggle to remain a place "where a family can eat without spending a fortune," as Stephen puts it.

Buoys, dock posts, and lobster-crate "chairs" lend this former truck garage a nautical air.

A Clam Cake Clam Primer

For years, the quahog was Rhode Island's best-selling commercial seafood and a big part of the Ocean State's identity, both comic and straight. (See Chapter 3 of this book for some of the comic.) Well before whites showed up, Narragansett and Wampanoag women gathered quahogs for roasting in campfires and steaming over earthen pits. In fact, the name quahog (pronounced co-hog and sometimes spelled quahaug) is derived from the Narragansett word *poquahock*, for round clam. And if you cross Water Street from Blount Clam Shack and Market in Warren, Rhode Island, in the early morning, you might be able to see individual commercial fishermen setting out in small boats for a morning of raking quahogs off the bottom of Narragansett Bay to sell to Andrade's Catch in Bristol, which sells to Blount's.

But their catch is not used in the clam cakes at Blount's or the majority of stands and restaurants in this book. Most instead use sea clams (also sometimes called surf or hen clams) for that.

First, some background. Clams come in two basic varieties: soft-shelled and hard-shelled. The soft-shelled are oval and only soft compared to the hard-shelled: brittle and thin are more like it. They are typically served steamed with melted butter (which is why they're sometimes called "steamers") or fried with their bellies attached and so are mainly of appeal to hard-core clam lovers.

Hard-shelled clams are, well, hard and circular, and come in sizes ranging from littlenecks (the smallest and sweetest and most expensive) to cherrystone (medium-sized) to quahog (the largest, toughest, and cheapest). Though confusingly enough, Rhode Islanders also use the term quahog generically for all hard-shelled clams.

Smaller hard-shelled clams are served raw on the half-shell or used in dishes like clams casino or linguini with clams. To mitigate their toughness, big quahogs are usually chopped up or minced before being put in stuffies or chowder (and for that reason are sometimes called chowders). But their flavor is usually considered too strong for clam cakes.

Enter sea clams. They're similar to quahogs in size, toughness, and hard-clam identity but are sweeter and traditionally cheaper. Nowadays, they're usually harvested by big dredging trawlers in the deep sea (hence their name) off the coasts of New Jersey and New York.

So sea clams are mostly not local to the East Coast clam fritter hot spots: This does not mean that they aren't good or fresh. Although sea clams make up most of the clams in cans, most of the best clam cake makers (i.e., most of the stands in this book) use fresh sea clams from a local purveyor like Tony's Seafood in Warren, Rhode Island. Fourth-generation fishmonger Mark Pirri of Tony's says clams you find in your favorite stand's clam cakes today could be as little as three days away from the ocean floor. The second day is taken up by hand or mechanical shucking; the third, with shipping the shucked meat from New Jersey or New York to New England. For the most part, Virginia fritter makers are still using local chowder clams.

How can you tell what kind of clam is in a clam cake purchased at a stand? Its color can provide a clue: Sea clams from the Atlantic Coast are orange or whitish yellow; ones from the Arctic bright red. Quahogs can look green or brown.

Black pieces in the clam cake dough are usually parts of bellies, meaning the restaurant uses a whole quahog or chowder clam. This is the norm with pancake-style clam fritters on the Eastern Shore of Virginia but highly unusual elsewhere.

The kind and quality of clams used are probably even more important in Maine, where the clam cakes are majority clam. But in the case of the RI-style clam cake that is merely flavored with seafood, the type of clam used probably matters less than how often the oil is changed or how much the kid on the clam cake fryer is paying attention to the cakes versus his cell phone.

It's the reason he and Michael moved the business from the pricy Newport waterfront to this unremarkable spot in 1998. Money was also behind their late 1980s switch from Atlantic to Pacific cod for their best-selling fish and chips.

As for the clam cakes, which are tennis-ball-sized and speckled with dark clam marks: He makes them with surf clams and Drum Rock. "I wish I could afford to do quahogs," he says. And he prefers Kenyon's mix to Drum Rock, but again, "It's too expensive."

Still, Stephen says, "I love working with food. I like banging out the chowders, stuffies, and lobster rolls like I just did this morning."

BLOUNT CLAM SHACKS
CLAM SHACK AND MARKET (YEAR-ROUND), 406 WATER ST., WARREN, RI, 401-245-1800; CLAM SHACK ON THE WATERFRONT (SEASONAL), 335 WATER ST., WARREN, RI, 401-245-3210; AND FOOD TRUCK; BLOUNTRETAIL.COM

Most of the clam cake makers in this book are little restaurants or shacks, or bigger restaurants that started out small.

A few are fish markets that started frying up some of their seafood as a convenience to customers.

But Blount's are the only clam cake shacks from a big company, albeit a big company that at least one historian credits for Rhode Islanders' love of quahog-flavored stuffies, chowder, and clam cakes.

Blount started out in 1880 as an oyster harvester but turned to quahogs after the 1938 hurricane destroyed most of Rhode Island's oyster beds. So late company president Nelson Blount's marketing efforts on behalf of the big, strongly flavored hard-shelled clam was an act of desperation with a happy ending.

The company changed course again at the turn of the twenty-first century: this time from selling quahogs and other clams to chowder makers like Campbell's, to making their own chowders and soups. Blount is, in fact, now America's largest maker of refrigerated soups.

Blount's year-round restaurant and market

So why does Blount Fine Foods run retail seafood shacks that probably only represent a tiny percentage of their overall business? "It's 1 percent of 1 percent," Nelson Blount's grandson, company president Todd Blount, clarifies, then explains, "It's a way to keep the family seafood brand alive. And I love clam shacks."

He loves them enough, in fact, to show up at the shack located across the street from the company's clam-processing-plant-turned-soup-factory to talk about them. During labor-starved 2021, Blount actually lured potential new plant hires with the promise of free Shack clam cakes and chowder for a year.

This cute little building is actually only one of two Blount Clam Shacks on Water Street in the company's original hometown of Warren. (Corporate offices moved to nearby Fall River, Massachusetts, in 2004.) This shack is year-round and resembles the mall and chain restaurants that use the company's soups in look and feel. It has attached fresh seafood and small gourmet markets where you can buy fresh fish or a frozen bag or refrigerated carton of your favorite soup or chowder to take home.

The other shack is summer-only and consists of two food trailers laid out in an L next to picnic tables—some under a big white catering tent—on the Warren River. There's free live music here on summer weekends.

Both shacks share a menu that shifts according to sales—as you might expect of any restaurant owned by a large company. For instance, when the year-round shack first opened, Blount recalled, "I said, 'We've got to have Rhode Island calamari!'"—but when sales stalled in the winter, off it went. And after opening with only the cold salad-style lobster roll traditional in Rhode Island, they've added a much-requested Connecticut-style hot-buttered option.

The clam cakes are Drum Rock standard-issue kicked up by the accompanying house-made spicy tarter.

If you live in New England, you've probably already had Blount's New England clam chowder: Blount is the largest maker of this style of chowder sold by restaurants, supermarkets, and delis in its region of origin—which is quite the endorsement.

Their Manhattan—with its still al dente potatoes and celery—might be even better. Their clambake chowder enlivens clear Rhode Island chowder with clambake ingredients like corn and chourico sausage.

Whichever variety you prefer, get a chowder with your clam cakes: The modern-day Blount success story was founded on them for a reason.

Shack Fries

One notable Blount Clam Shack menu item is Shack Fries. They're essentially seafood nachos and a fun way for a group to start a meal there. Here's the Blount recipe for making them.

4 large sea scallops, breaded and deep fried

4 large shrimp, shelled, deveined, battered, and deep fried

10 ounces cooked French fries (about 50 standard-sized fries)

1 cup New England-style clam chowder, heated

¼ cup sharp cheddar cheese (preferably white), shredded

2 to 3 scallions, chopped

Purchase from a restaurant, bake from frozen, or fry the scallops, shrimp, and French fries in that order. Set the fish aside. Place the hot fries on a small platter, then cover with cheese, hot clam chowder, and the scallops and shrimp. Garnish with scallions. Serve hot.

Blount's Shack Fries

Yield: 2 to 3 servings

Off Track?

Former Blount Seafood president Nelson Blount was a big rail buff, and in 1955, he bought a floundering Carver, Massachusetts, narrow-gauge railroad started by a distant cousin. Throughout the 1950s and 1960s, some Blount employees would show up for work unsure if they'd be spending the day on the clam line or the train gang.

Though Blount sold Edaville Railroad in 1970, it remains a favorite family day-trip destination to this day.

CAP'N JACK'S RESTAURANT
706 SUCCOTASH RD., WAKEFIELD, RI, 401-789-4556,
CAPNJACKSRESTAURANT.COM

Drive down sleepy Succotash Road in Wakefield, Rhode Island, on almost any early summer evening, and you'll see cars stacked up on the side of the road near the Jerusalem bridge like planes on a runway, sometimes with a cop directing traffic.

What's causing all the excitement? Freshly showered and spiffed-up people waiting for their valet-parking turn to eat quinoa crab salad, togarashi scallops, and Potter Pond poke at the Matunuck Oyster House, one of the buzziest seafood restaurants in South County Rhode Island, despite their lack of clam cakes.

Meanwhile, diagonally across the street, boisterous families in bathing suits pile out of cars with no police assistance to sit down at long tables and chow down on clam cakes and fish and chips at Cap'n Jack's, a full-service restaurant as comfortable as an old boat shoe.

Cap'n Jack's is, in fact, probably the closest thing to eating at one of the state's famed amusement park shore dinner halls, circa the early 1970s, as anyone can today experience. That is actually when Pete Piemonte and his son, restaurant namesake Jack, turned this former little lunch stand into a sprawling, sit-down seafood restaurant overlooking the Succotash Salt Marsh.

From the outside, with its port holes and faux top deck, the building resembles a beached cruise ship. The nautical theme continues inside, but with restraint. A few ship's pictures and nautical lamps aside, the "decor" is plain wooden tables, floors, and walls.

The food is similarly straightforward.

Asked to identify must-eats from the 50-item menu, third-generation owner Jack Piemonte Jr. does not hesitate: "Chowder, clam cakes, and fish and chips."

The clam cakes are among the most flavorful in the state. Could it be because Cap'n Jack's clam cake recipe's only liquid is clam juice instead of the usual water or a mix of both? Piemonte thinks their flour is the game-changer: They use a 50/50 blend of cake and bread flour, versus the more common all-purpose flour or Drum Rock mix.

Piemonte also swears by Clabber Girl baking powder. And his best-selling beer-batter haddock is made only with plebian Budweiser. Cap'n Jack's also makes their own chowders: Rhode Island clear and New England-style milk.

Whatever you order, consider sharing. Portions are generous to gigantic, and you want to have room for the desserts, which are also huge, homemade, and good enough for this to be a dessert destination. (Among well-known clam cake eateries, only Aunt Carrie's and the Lobster Shack at Two Lights can make a similar claim.)

Restaurant founder Pete was a baker and the creator of the recipes for their apple turnovers, Grape-Nuts pudding, carrot cake, and pies that Piemonte's mom, Martha, now makes along with her own popular lemon-coconut-raspberry cake and apple caramel bash (apple pie topped with cubes of butterscotch brownies covered in caramel sauce). Her chocolate éclairs are so big that

The north-end patio of Cap'n Jack's, overlooking Succotash Salt Marsh

some seniors take them home and make them dessert for the week.

Martha met Jack Piemonte Sr. while waitressing at Cap'n Jack's, and both their kids started helping out there while still in grammar school. Martha insisted they go to college to expand their minds and options. But her son's choices of hospitality management at the University of New Hampshire and culinary arts at the Culinary Institute of America were more about focus.

"I always knew I wanted to work here," he says. Fast-talking, friendly, and as naturally sunny as his grandfather was famously grouchy, Piemonte finds it easy to explain why, including the work's variety, autonomy, and local focus.

Regulars—both locals and visitors who rent the same cottages every summer—make up such a big part of their business that "Friday nights here is like dinner with friends," Piemonte says. Though there is the parallel downside "when people who knew my grandfather say they remember when clam cakes were a nickel and want to know why I'm charging more."

Yet Another Reason to Go to Cap'n Jack's (That Has Nothing to Do with Food)

Rhode Island native and ex-Army infantryman Angel Gomez lost his right leg when his Humvee was bombed during the Iraq War. While Gomez was recovering from multiple surgeries at Fort Sam Houston in San Antonio, Texas, Rhode Island fishing buddy Alex MacLeod called to ask if there was anything he could do.

"All I could think is that I wanted some clam cakes," Gomez told the *Westerly Sun*'s Michael Souza in 2011.

MacLeod called around to local restaurants, trying to make it happen, and he got the runaround from every one but Cap'n Jack's. "They said, 'Give us a few minutes.' Five minutes later they called back and said it was no trouble," MacLeod said.

It wasn't long before Gomez had enough clam cakes and chowder to feed his whole hospital ward.

New England's Nutty Dessert

Grape-Nuts cereal is weird enough: It's made of neither grapes nor nuts but rather twice-baked whole wheat and malted barley bread crumbs that the cereal's creator, C.W. Post, likened to nuts with a grape-sugary taste.

Weirder still are the malty sweet Grape-Nuts desserts you've likely encountered during your visits to New England stands profiled in this book: Grape-Nuts pudding at Lobster Shack at Two Lights, Evelyn's, and Cap'n Jack's, and Grape-Nuts ice cream at Gray's.

Post was a cereal and food-marketing pioneer, who served Post plant tour visitors Grape-Nuts ice cream within a few years of the cereal's 1898 debut and put a pudding recipe on the box a few years after that.

That plant was in Battle Creek, Michigan, and Grape-Nuts was never a New England-only food. So why do Grape-Nuts desserts show up at low-brow eateries and ice cream stands there and almost nowhere else in the country?

Current Grape-Nuts officials declined the opportunity to weigh in. But a search of the *Chronicling America* historic newspaper archives shows that the cereal's initial advertising campaign was launched in the Connecticut, Maine, and Washington, DC, markets.

So this could be a case of the oldest habits being the most in-grained (pun intended).

You can get Grape-Nuts pudding at Cap'n Jack's and some New England diners and luncheonettes year-round. Those who only visit New England in the summer can get their off-season fix using the following recipe.

Grape-Nuts Pudding

1 cup Grape-Nuts cereal

¼ cup butter, melted

3 eggs, well beaten

½ cup sugar

2 cups milk

1 ½ teaspoons vanilla

⅛ teaspoon salt

⅛ teaspoon nutmeg

Preheat oven to 375°F. Grease a one-quart baking dish. Sprinkle a layer of Grape-Nuts on the bottom of the dish. In a small bowl, blend remaining cereal with butter. In a medium bowl, beat sugar into the eggs. Add cereal/butter mixture to the larger bowl with the sugary eggs, then blend in milk, vanilla, and salt. Pour into casserole dish.

Place casserole dish in a larger dish of hot water and put in the oven. Bake uncovered for 30 minutes, then stir the custard and sprinkle the top with the nutmeg. Return to the oven and bake another 20 minutes or until pudding is softly set and a knife inserted in the center comes out clean.

Yield: 6 servings

CHAMPLIN'S SEAFOOD DECK
256 GREAT ISLAND RD., NARRAGANSETT, RI, 401-783-3152,
CHAMPLINS.COM

Best not to know what goes on behind the scenes at most businesses. But what most customers of Champlin's Seafood Deck don't see is as impressive as what they do.

Showing up at Champlin's first-floor seafood market to talk to owner Robert Mitchell Sr., I was led through a back door and toward the docks through a room filled with the sound of running water and lined with wooden tanks of live lobster and crab.

In a later interview, Mitchell's son, Robert Jr., estimated that 95 percent of the seafood being eaten in the restaurant above came off these docks and through this room, where fish are filleted and clams are shucked hours to a few days from the catch.

In fact, if you go by sales, Champlin's is mainly a wholesale and retail fish market. And it is not alone among clam cake makers in having that dual role. (See pp. 39 and 41 for others.)

But it is the only clam-cake-making fish market in this book with a dockside channel location affording an up-close-and-personal view of Rhode Island's largest fishing fleet. (In fact, Champlin's Galilee home is Rhode Island's busiest commercial fishing port.) Those with less piscine interests will enjoy checking out the fashion statements on the ferries going to and from Block Island. (Yes, you'll be almost close enough to read the labels.)

Champlin's was only a little fish shack when it opened on this spot in the 1920s, with a few prepared foods like

At Champlin's, you can eat seafood in sight of the boats that delivered it.

chowder and lobster rolls offered in the 1930s and 1940s. Putting the restaurant on the second story was the Champlin family's logical response to losing several previous buildings to hurricanes (though it also makes this place very handicapped unfriendly).

On busy summer Saturdays, the line from the ordering window extends down those outdoor stairs to the ground, thus creating a bit of Soup Nazi-like pressure when it's finally your turn. It's smart to spend the waiting time studying one of the paper menus that lists all the options and also answers frequently asked questions like whether you can make substitutions on the seafood platter or clambake (no), why some guy with a lower number got his order before yours ("Some orders . . . take longer"), and what kind of coating is on the fish and chips (dry breading—"not wet and puffed").

According to Mitchell, 95 percent of people ordering the fish and chips choose flounder over haddock, and you should too: It's from right there in Galilee instead of New Bedford. A couple of other things the menu doesn't tell you: The chowders (white, red, and clear) and clam cakes are both made with a mix of quahog and sea clams. Minced quahogs are there for flavor, and because it disappears into the dough, chopped sea clams are used so people can see there's some clam.

Fish and chips, clam cakes, chowder, and fried clams: These basics are the best-sellers. All have straightforward preparations, using Drum Rock mixes.

More unusual offerings include old-fashioned fish cakes and snail salad. The latter excuse to eat copious amounts of garlic features marinated local conch and is "very Italian," according to Mitchell, whose family bought the business from the Champlins with several other partners in 1990. Moreover, Champlin's the restaurant will prepare any big lobster you pick out from the tank in their fish market for a nominal additional fee.

After ordering, you and other members of your dining party should fan out and access the possibilities from among Champlin's many seating options.

These include water-level picnic tables, an indoor wooden dining room, and covered and uncovered decks with and without water views. Numbers can be heard anywhere on the second floor, and on a busy night, it's smart to see who's almost finished eating so you can be ready to pounce. (My favorite spot is a small, uncovered ledge on the north side of the building overlooking some docked fishing boats.)

This is not even to mention the competition for parking at one of Champlin's 12 spaces or at the small free public lot across the street. Many people give up and park in one of the $10 Block Island ferry lots.

Champlin's is dock-to-dinner with a free-for-all cafeteria atmosphere. Those looking for valet parking, waiter or waitress service, and a kitchen with a chef rather than a cook might want to go across the street to George's.

DUNE BROTHERS
239 DYER ST., PROVIDENCE, RI, 401-480-1269, DUNEBROTHERS.COM

Local sourcing. Social media savvy. Food trailer or truck-based.

Dune Brothers is the only Southern New England seafood takeout that checks all these of-the-moment boxes.

Instead of making fish and chips from the standard haddock or cod, Dune Brothers offers a rotating selection of three lesser-known fish caught off local waters. One recent day it was pollock, skate, and dogfish (aka Cape shark).

"It's better for fishermen not to have to ship their catch overseas and more affordable for us," explains Jason Hegedus, sitting at a table in Dune Brothers' picnic area one fall morning in hipster-regulation hoodie and beanie.

Dune Brothers is one of the few city clam cake makers.

Sustainability is on the menu at Dune.

But it means he and his baseball-cap-adorned, bearded brother-in-fish Nicholas Gillespie spend almost as much time talking about their food as they do cooking it. Hegedus actually has pictures of dogfish on his phone to show wary customers that they're not cooking Fido.

More conventional offerings like clams and lobster are also all from New England.

"Everyone's familiar with farm to table; we're doing pier to plate," Gillespie says.

The pair's shack fare is also informed and elevated by their time on the lines of fancy restaurants (Hegedus at Blue Hill in Manhattan; Gillespie at Salts in Cambridge, Massachusetts).

Their hot-buttered lobster rolls aren't just doused in melted butter but gently tossed with a warm *beurre monté* butter *sauce*; the bread-and-butter pickles on their fish sandwich are made in the trailer from fresh cucumber; and they proudly fry all their seafood in beef fat. "It tastes better" and is what the UK fish and chipperies they admire use, Gillespie says.

Given all that, you might assume Dune Brothers' clam cakes would be made from scratch. But no, actually, they use commercial Drum Rock.

"It's great, it's local, and it's tried-and-true," Gillespie says, a bit defensively, adding that the Drum Rock mix is only the beginning—they do a lot of things to it to make their clam cakes their own.

He is not kidding. Their clam balls are baseball-sized, redolent of quahog juice and French *fines herbes* flavor, and oozing with orange grease. They are less New England clam cake than Indian street food, especially when dipped in the brothers' own curry ketchup.

Their clam chowder—with its salt pork and fresh Narragansett Bay quahog base and crouton topping—is also like no other shack's, tasting like a cross between New England white chowder and onion soup.

Native Rhode Islander Hegedus and Massachusetts man Gillespie started seriously messing around with food expectations as fellow students at the New England Culinary Institute. They became reacquainted in 2015 when both got restaurant jobs in Portland, Oregon (aka the hipster capital of America).

The pair cooked up the idea of doing a seafood shack pop-up one night while reminiscing about their respective New England childhood summers over beers and fried smelts. That side project's success led them to wonder where they could do the same thing full-time and, at the time, "No one else was doing shack food in Providence," says Hegedus.

Almost no one else was working in Providence's Jewelry District when Dune Brothers opened there in 2017 either. Today, their bright red faux clam shack trailer sits across from a park, Brown University's School of Professional Studies and Medical School, and the Cambridge Innovation Center incubator that, together with frequent social media postings, fill their picnic tables.

Hegedus recalled one Instagram poster who had just landed at Green airport expressing surprise that his online search for best seafood in the state had him driving away from the shore and into Providence.

In fact, business has been so good that the Dune brothers have had to take the fresh oysters and grilled whole fish off the regular menu. "There is only so much you can do in a 20-foot trailer," Hegedus explains.

The pair hope to solve that problem with a planned year-round space in Providence and more shacks bringing Indian-style clam cakes to a neighborhood near you.

EVELYN'S DRIVE-IN
2335 MAIN RD., TIVERTON, RI, 401-624-3100,
EVELYNSDRIVEIN.COM

Sitting at a Nanaquaket Pond-side picnic table at Evelyn's eating clam cakes one perfect late July day and what popped into my mind was not "Where's the tartar?"—it was right there, though hardly necessary—but Psalm 23:

> *The Lord is my shepherd*
> *I shall not want*
> *He maketh me order the golden clam cakes*
> *He leadeth me beside the still waters*
> *He restoreth my soul.*

There might be better clam cakes in Rhode Island (some would dispute it), and there are certainly cake-making shacks where the water views are even more spectacular (Monahan's in Narragansett, Rhode Island, and Lobster Shack at Two Lights in Port Elizabeth, Maine, come to mind) but none that are more peaceful than Evelyn's. That is, assuming you visit during off-hours or have already put in your time on line.

Evelyn DuPont opened this business in 1969 as a takeout stand selling fried seafood, later tacking part of a Main Street, Tiverton, house to the back along with indoor seating and diner-style dishes.

The current and only second owners, Domenic and Jane Bitto, took over in 1987—the result of a wrong turn that turned out to be just right. "I was on my way to look at a restaurant for sale on the Cape but got hopelessly lost and missed the appointment," Dom recalls. He stopped to ask where he could get a bite to eat, and the suggestion was Evelyn's. While chowing down on a burger and fries, he learned the place was for sale.

The Bittos assumed ownership as newlyweds and at the beginning of a Fourth of July weekend (i.e., the busiest possible time). DuPont had agreed to stay for two months to teach them the ropes, but "after a month, we let her go," says Domenic.

"There were no recipes, just Evelyn saying, 'You take a handful of this . . . ' and 24-year-old me with pen in hand, trying to get it all down and wondering, 'Whose hand does she mean? Mine or hers? Cause mine is lots bigger. . . .' And she'd take over when we got in trouble, which didn't seem like it would be helpful in the long run. I lost a lot of hair that summer I'll tell you."

Eventually, though, the Bittos were as in love with the business as they were with each other. That explains why they've changed so little—keeping the old-fashioned picnic pavilion, Evelyn's addition (with Main Street address still visible), and the Coke sign (though they now serve Pepsi). They've also stayed true to Evelyn's recipes to the extent they could figure them out.

All the fried seafood is breaded rather than battered, a style of preparation that requires changing the oil daily, "which is more expensive," Domenic points out. But they do it anyway.

Some non-seafood items from Evelyn's diner days, like chicken pot pie, appear as weekly specials. Grape-Nuts pudding, chicken, beef, and vegetarian chow mein, and their Rhode Island corollary, chow mein sandwiches (see side story) are served every day alongside lobster chow mein, a high-brow-meets-low Jane creation that was featured on *Diners, Drive-Ins and Dives* and is now all over the Internet.

How do they feel about being known for a stunt dish?

"We're known for our fried clams," the unflappable, ever-affable Domenic replies.

Also for their clam cakes, which *New England Clam Shack Cookbook* author Brooke Dojny called "the best I've ever eaten." DuPont only made them on weekends, but the Bittos make a fresh batch from Evelyn-favored Drum Rock mix (but with double the amount of Evelyn-specified clams) at least once a day because "yeast batters don't do well refrigerated," Domenic says.

Evelyn's holds a contest every June to see which of the new batch of summer employees can make clam cakes the fastest while still maintaining standards of tennis-ball-sized, uniform shape, golden color, and hot temperature.

Many of the items the Bittos added to the menu are healthier, grilled ones, like Domenic's sea scallops with lemon, thyme, and garlic. Other Bitto innovations—a VW Beetle that ran on their used cooking oil (now unrelatedly defunct), a long-running concert series benefiting local food banks, garden "peace pole," and a menu-printed commitment to "generously providing care, love and kindness to all we encounter"—lend a positive, New Agey vibe.

Dom definitely seems like a glass-half-full kind of guy. Asked about a 2005 fire that closed Evelyn's for almost a year and a half and he talks about resulting upgrades that quadrupled cooking capacity. Similarly, he says the pandemic increased business and led them to buy a tent that expanded their already wide seating choices.

As for the post-Jane-and-Dom era: Domenic says, "If anyone from the family takes it over, it will be her," pointing to his daughter, Jesse, waiting on a nearby table.

Asked about this later—the lunch rush being over, Jesse was now in a swimsuit on her way to the pond for a quick pre-dinner paddle, she replies, "Who would want to leave this little piece of paradise?" with only the slightest hint of an ironic smile.

Evelyn on Evelyn's

The idea had been to eat at Evelyn's with former owner and namesake Evelyn DuPont and get her review of the place today.

It was not to be, as Evelyn, 88, is now living in a Florida nursing facility.

But she has eaten at her old restaurant several times since moving to warmer climes, including once within the last half-decade, and was happy to talk on the phone.

"I think [current owners Jane and Domenic Bitto] are doing a good job. It's fine. Whatever I told them to do, they did it. . . . They're a good couple. I'm glad I sold it to them," she says.

As for her memories of the clam cakes back when she made them, they're not entirely positive.

"They were a pain in the neck. They had their own batter you had to make, and they had to have their own fryolator."

Did she eat them?

"Not really. We always had fried clams. That was the main thing. That and shrimp." Which she would eat "once in a while," she says without enthusiasm.

So what food does this Rhode Island seafood shack icon like?

"Steak!"

"My husband started the business for me," she continues after a moment. "He had money. I didn't." But he was never involved in the day-to-day: His personality was ill-suited for it, she says.

Evelyn's founder, Evelyn DuPont, in her drive-in in the mid-1970s, penciled-in eyebrows courtesy of an earlier fryer accident

"He was a very nervous person. He loved racing. So I'd send him to the race track. I remember once one woman said to me, 'He's out there enjoying himself, and you're in here working your ass off.' I said, 'That's my business.'

"I knew he wanted to be there [at the track]. And I didn't care. I enjoyed working. I had a lot of fun in that place."

Gray's for Dessert

There are only four desserts at Evelyn's. It seems Evelyn's has ceded that part of their menu to **Gray's** (16 East Rd., Tiverton, RI, 401-624-4500, www.grays icecream.com), one of Rhode Island's premiere ice cream destinations, only a five-minute drive away.

Annie Gray started selling ice cream from her house on the site of what is now Gray's parking lot 100 years ago, and most of the must-haves of the 40 high-fat, house-made flavors are old-fashioned ones you can't get elsewhere: maple walnut, Indian pudding, rum raisin, frozen pudding, Grape-Nuts, and ginger (made with real ginger root) among them.

The stand's eccentricity doesn't end with their flavors. Gray's is three times the size of the usual ice cream stand and opens at 7 a.m. 365 days a year. In part that's because the back of the building houses a corner store, in case you want some Campbell's soup along with your morning coffee cone.

Although Gray's can serve up to 4,000 on a busy summer Sunday, it has only two covered picnic tables: Most people eat their ice cream by the shade of giant trees on the stone wall that separates Gray's from the historic Chace-Cory House next door. Its grounds sports a wooden cutout of a cow (its connection to Gray's unclear). Gray's owner, Marilyn Bettencourt, used to keep a few real cows for the visiting kids (versus for their milk) until 2014, when a calf named Oreo bit someone, and that was the end of that.

Chow Mein Rollin' in Fall River

Is the chow mein sandwich Greek to you? Then you probably didn't grow up in Fall River, Massachusetts, or nearby Rhode Island between 1920 and 1990, when these sandwiches were served not just in Chinese restaurants but also many lunch counters, school and factory cafeterias, and even some drive-ins like Evelyn's.

It's basically chow mein on a hamburger bun, a big sloppy mess either wrapped in wax paper to-go or piled overflowing on a plate and eaten with knife and fork.

Chinese restaurateurs in Fall River invented them as a way to make the already culturally watered-down dish of sauce-covered fried noodles into a quick and cheap lunch for the city's factory workers. And then others copied, says Imogene Lim, who parlayed her chow mein scholarship into a professorship at Vancouver Island University.

Lim, the Bittos of Evelyn's, and Emeril Lagasse (who ate a chow mein sandwich weekly growing up in Fall River) agree that the best chow mein sandwiches are made with Hoo-Mee noodles from the 85-year-old Oriental Chow Mein Company of Fall River.

Home cooks can buy Hoo-Mee noodles packaged in an unselfconsciously retro yellow box with dried gravy mix in Southern New England supermarkets or from the New England specialty site www.famousfoods.com.

FLO'S CLAM SHACK AND DRIVE-IN
4 WAVE AVE., MIDDLETOWN, RI, AND PARK AVENUE,
ISLAND BEACH PARK, PORTSMOUTH, RI, 401-847-8141,
FLOSCLAMSHACKS.COM

Even the most interesting New England clam shacks are a bit sedate. Reservedness goes with the Yankee territory.

This is not the case at Flo's. Their Middletown, Rhode Island, shack doubles as a museum of tacky marine tchotchkes and Rhode Island pop culture curated by outsized owner Komes Rozes. Multiple prizes for their clam cakes, fried clams, and fish and chips can mean long lines. But there's so much to look at almost nobody minds.

"People bring me things," he says in response to a question about where all the license plates, photographs, and life preservers hanging from the walls and ceilings come from. Or people tell him about things.

The 25-foot shark statue out front that originally topped a Cranston nightclub, for instance, bid up to $1,200 on Facebook Marketplace until Rozes got wind and ended the auction with a cash offer of $2,000.

Entertaining a visitor from his perch at a stool at the second-floor bar, an entourage of relatives and friends in tow and employees hustling to fulfill his every desire, Rozes is gleeful ringmaster presiding over a restaurant circus. There's even a funhouse mirror (though its placement beside the indoor ordering counter seems unwise).

The giant outdoor shark is only the beginning of the fun at Flo's Middletown.

This is not the original Flo's, and Rozes is not Flo's original owner. That would be Flora Helger, who, in 1936, dragged an old chicken coop to a spot across the street from the Sakonnet River some 10 miles north of the Middletown Flo's to sell clam cakes and fried clams to-go. Fast-forward to 1978: Flo is ready to call it a career, and Florida seafood restaurant manager Rozes wants to relocate to his native Rhode Island.

At that point, Flo's was still little more than an ordering window and some picnic tables, albeit one so locally renowned as to cause weekend traffic jams. Rozes was astonished on the stormy day he went to check the place out to see people standing in line in the rain.

That simple shack is still there offering that same kind of laid-back clam shack experience. (It's not exactly the *same* shack but one like it—the shack has been rebuilt multiple times because of hurricanes.) It's still takeout only (in Chinese restaurant cartons) of the small original menu of fried clams, fish and chips, and clam cakes.

The key to the clam cakes' popularity is "Narragansett Bay quahogs—it gives the best flavor," Rozes says. Flo's cakes and chowder contain both their ground-up meat and juice. He says his clam cakes are also lighter and fluffier than others: He knows because he makes an annual tour of competitors. This leads him to wonder aloud why the clam cake raters known as the Clamarati have never been to Flo's Middletown.

"One time they said they tried but the line was too long. But this is a restaurant, not a bus stop. It's not fair!" he protests, as the bartender, his girlfriend, and his son murmur their assent.

Flo's sells the most clam cakes to "people who don't like seafood—they don't have an overpowering fishy flavor" and also at the more demur Portsmouth stand, which is patronized largely by locals.

"For almost 70 years that place was like a tradition, a secret that nobody else knew about," Rozes recalls.

And what businessman wants his business to be secret?

And so when Hurricane Bob blew through Rhode Island's East Bay in 1991, leaving behind only the Flo's Drive-In sign, Rozes didn't just rebuild the original Flo's: He bought another building on busy, touristy Ocean Avenue in Middletown that had withstood the great New England hurricane of 1938 and every one after to be his second Flo's.

It has a better water view, indoor and outdoor seating, regular and raw bars, and is the showplace for Rozes's most interesting and fun ideas, like the aforementioned giant shark, the nod-to-McDonald's "Over 40 million clam cakes served" sign, and the front patio festooned to look like Gilligan's Island's lagoon, complete with palm trees. Middletown's menu is also bigger, featuring a $90 "gourmet"-hot-dog-and-Moet-champagne special and the "Rhode Island Lunch" hot cheese sandwich. The latter is an obscure regional specialty consisting of melted cheese sauce on a toasted hamburger bun topped with mustard, onion, and relish that Rozes's uncle sold at his now-defunct Rhode Island Lunch diner in Newport. Says Rozes, "It was supposed to be a hangover cure for partying Newport Naval officers. It's like a grilled cheese, only better."

For many years, both Flo's handed out beach stones with colorful painted-on numbers instead of order tickets that Rozes also sold as souvenirs. (If there's another way to make a buck, Rozes will think of it.) But when Portsmouth neighbors complained about having to listen to the numbers being called out on the public address, Rozes switched to lobster-shaped pagers so fragile they hardly lasted a season.

In summer 2021, Kozes was using plain old rectangular pagers, and he was not happy about it. By the time you read this, he'll doubtless have come up with something much more interesting and fun.

> ►► If the lines are too long at Flo's Drive-In, you might want to drive a few hundred feet up the road to **Schultzy's Snack Shack** (346 Park Ave., Portsmouth, RI, 401-683-2663, schultzyssnackshack.com). Schultzy's has none of Flo's nautical salvage charm but plenty of compensating kitchen cred: Before buying this place in 2013, Schultzy's chef-owner Kurt Schultz cooked at a number of high-end Newport-area spots (like the Atlantic Beach Club) and for Jackie Kennedy Onassis's mother, Janet Auchincloss (although he allows it was only at the end of her life when her main concern was that "everything look beautiful"). Schultz developed his clam cake recipe at one of his fancy restaurant gigs, and it's different from Flo's and the usual in containing corn flour and scallion and thus evoking thoughts of crispy scallion pancakes and Lipton Onion Soup mix. Insider diet tip: Although it's not on the menu, Schultzy's will sell you a single clam cake with a cup of chowder in addition to the usual dozen or half-dozen.

GEORGE'S OF GALILEE
250 SAND HILL COVE RD., NARRAGANSETT, RI, 401-783-2306,
GEORGESOFGALILEE.COM

George's of Galilee has long been known as the clam cake place for partiers. Disembark from the Block Island Ferry late on a Friday or Saturday summer evening and it will be to music and raucous laughter from George's.

Street view of George's

But George's is actually much bigger than this one image, I discovered when visiting one summer weekday to try their clam cakes, which are much better than necessary to please a drunkard. George's is, rather, about five restaurants in one, and your image of it will depend on when you visit and where you sit.

Yes, at peak times during the summer, George's could have up to six bars going.

But they also have a front patio with fire pits, a takeout stand by the parking lot, an indoor dining room with a fireplace, an enclosed porch with a view of the channel boat traffic, and an outdoor one overlooking their beach.

You read that right, George's has its own beach abutting the state one, with its own *free* parking, although, general manager and executive chef Yulia Kuzmina says, "It fills up pretty quick in the morning." Clam cakes for breakfast? Why not?

Like many of the businesses in this book, George's started out as a little lunch shack—in this case, run by one George Hazard in the 1930s. This was when Galilee was mainly a fishing village rather than a place for tourists to park and eat on the way to or from the beach and Block Island.

But unlike most clam shacks, George's kept growing, with additions and renovations that turned the shack into a sprawling building. Purchased by George's bread deliveryman Norman Durfee in 1948 and now owned by Norman's grandson, Kevin, George's has almost 500 seats, making it one of Rhode Island's largest restaurants, and the town of Narragansett's second-largest employer.

By dint of its age and size, George's has achieved the level of institution in South County, Rhode Island, so much so that staff regularly fields phone calls asking "about the weather, the [Block Island] ferry schedule, and what they're charging for lobster at [competitor] Champlin's. We're like a free information station," Kuzmina says with a rueful laugh.

And yet field them they do. With 250 employees during the peak summer season, George's has the people to (politely) handle it. Their staff also wait on you, a refreshing change from a steady diet of takeout that has become ubiquitous post-pandemic.

Does George's feel corporate? A little. Does this mean cooking by Cisco? Kuzmina says no. "We cook from scratch with nothing premade."

That includes the three-inch clam cakes, which are made with chopped sea clams that appear as black spots on the crust and orange pieces in the pillowy dough. They come to the table hot and crunchy, full of clam and other satisfying flavors. Most people order them with George's Rhode Island-style clear chowder, also house-made and featuring a mix of sea clams and the more flavorful quahog.

The traditional clam cakes and chowder, fried clams, fish and chips, and lobster rolls are frequent award-winners and best-sellers even as George's has expanded its menu to include healthier preparations of more sustainable— though less familiar—fish like fluke, scup, and sea robin. "We support the

Rick Browne and the Mystery of the Migrating Clams

For every Southern New England clam shack customer who complains about the lack of clams in their clam cakes, there are five clam shack owners who insist that they do, too, put lots of clams in their clam cake batter: People only think they don't because of how many of those clam pieces end up as burnt spots on the clam cakes' surface, and not so obviously a piece of clam.

Look at almost any Rhode Island-style clam cake (and most pictures of some herein) and you'll see that this is not just an excuse but something that actually does happen. But why does it happen, and is there any way to keep the clam pieces in the dough, tasting and looking like clam?

Presented this question, frying expert Rick Browne (*The Frequent Fryers Cookbook*, *The Ultimate Guide to Frying*) likened it to raisins in cakes sinking to the bottom of the pan and suggested borrowing the same time-honored solution: Covering the raisins—or in the case of clam cakes, the clam pieces—with a very light coating of flour.

"The clams are wet, slippery, and smooth, so when they heat up, they move. The flour binds them to keep them in the middle."

Though this was only Browne's theory—he lives in Oregon, far from clam cake land—it proved true when tested in my kitchen (the uncoated clams in a half-batch spotted the clam cake surfaces; the coated ones put in the other half-batch stayed in the dough after cooking). It's the scientific principle of friction or resistance in action, according to University of Rhode Island food scientist Chong Lee.

So clam shack owners, there is a solution if you're willing to go to the extra trouble of flouring your clam pieces.

fisherman by buying whatever they catch," says Kuzmina. "They literally walk across the street to deliver to us."

Another George's plus: superior clam cake merchandise, including a George's clam cake sack holiday tree ornament and infant T-shirts boasting, "I just had my first clam cake at George's."

And if George's keeps to current standards, this clam cake first-timer will likely be back: for a night of drinking as a young adult, a takeout beach snack with the kids as a parent, and a rainy day lunch of clam cakes and chowder by the fire as a senior citizen.

HITCHING POST RESTAURANT
5402 POST RD., CHARLESTOWN, RI, 401-364-7495,
HITCHINGPOSTRI.COM

"Home of the World Famous Clam Fritter" read the signs at the Hitching Post. Well, maybe. Ask a local to name their favorite clam cake spots and the Hitching Post probably won't come up—possibly because of their almost-in-Connecticut location or how here, they're not even called clam cakes.

Even Hitching Post owner Tammy Duhamel McLellan was surprised when her stand topped the Clamarati tester's 2017 ranking of the state's best clam cakes. Not because she doesn't think her fritters deserving or well-known, but because she received no official notification or prize.

"We only found out about it because people started coming in saying that they saw we had won and wanted to come try them," says McLellan, a smile only partly masking mild annoyance.

But this quiet little place's fritters were Westerly, Rhode Island-famous decades before the Clamarati came.

In the 1940s, McLellan's grandfather, Edward Duhamel, owned a full-service restaurant called The Willows that became known for its clam fritters—so much so that in 1950, Ed decided to open a takeout stand nearby to keep the takeout fritter customers from clogging up his kitchen. As a teenager, McLellan's father, Jerry, used to commute to his job at the stand by horse, hence the Hitching Post name.

Ed and Jerry are both now long gone but are celebrated in family photos that decorate the Hitching Post's small indoor dining area and restaurant merchandise case, the latter offering T-shirts that frame Jerry Duhamel as Rhode Island seafood's Ray Kroc. Eating in there also offers the possibility of being waited on by the daughter of this local junk-food icon.

But unless it's raining or very hot, most people opt for outdoor dining at patio or picnic tables (including mini ones for the kids) in a grassy area to the side or in the lovely garden out back. Yelpers praise the Hitching Post's park-like environs as much if not more than the clam fritters, hand-cut onion rings, and local Warwick ice cream and shakes.

The fritters are notable in several ways: One, obviously, is in the fritter name. This is common in Connecticut but almost unheard of in contemporary Rhode Island, McLellan is reminded on an almost daily basis. Although this was not McClellan's doing, it is a family legacy that she defends in countless, sometimes contentious, customer conversations.

"Something that's leavened and deep fried is a fritter. Apple fritters would be another example. Whereas a cake is flat and pan-fried on the griddle, like jonnycakes," McLellan explains, sounding very much like the schoolteacher she is nine months of the year. "But a lot of people just don't want to hear it."

Secondly, the Hitching Post's clam cakes—err, fritters—have the distinctive airy texture of a French doughnut and are lighter than competitors'. At least, that's what McLellan has been told—she's never tried anybody else's. "Why bother when we make the best?" she reasons.

Is there cornmeal in there? McLellan shakes her head no. She demonstrates how she minces the quahogs she uses for the fritters and her Rhode Island clear chowder with an old-fashioned hand grinder. Beyond that, the recipe is a secret, today known only to the two living souls who make them: McLellan and her husband, Timothy, also a teacher.

It's a profession that comes in handy for obtaining and training a staff of high schoolers.

"We know how to deal with kids. One girl who used to work for us is now running a pizza place," she notes proudly.

As for her own kids: McLellan's plan to pass the stand along to her daughter was foiled when Tiffany fell for a Floridian.

So what happens when she's had enough of explaining fritters?

"Maybe I'll lease it out to a hair salon," McLellan muses aloud.

Really? Just put a fork in a 70-plus-year-old family restaurant?

"I'd rather go out on top than see it run by someone not up to my standards," she says.

Update: In summer 2022, the Hitching Post operated as a landlocked outpost of Monahan's Clam Shack by the Sea while Tammy McLellan recovered from injuries suffered in an off-season car accident—thus casting the future of the Hitching Post as a beachhead of RI clam fritter advocacy in doubt.

>> If you feel like you can not, in good conscience, patronize a Rhode Island clam shack that calls their clam cakes fritters, you might want to drive 6 miles down the road to **N.O. Bar Clam Shack** (523 Charlestown Beach Rd., Charlestown, RI, 401-409-1151, nobarclamshack.com). Connecticut Italian restaurant owner Rich Nemarich took over the former Johnny Angels clam shack in 2021 and renamed it N.O. after the Ninigret Pond oysters that are farmed just off the dock of their Shelter Cove Marina home—although there are no oysters on the largely fried seafood menu. As if this wasn't confusing enough, "N.O. Bar" Clam Shack has a full liquor license. Connecticut native Nemarich and Yemeni chef Saleem Nassir also

have a combined zero years of experience making and selling fried sea-food. Despite this, or maybe because of it, they've come up with a killer original recipe producing a clam cake with a golden color, great crunch, and, most importantly, a fine-crumbed, feather-light inside that actually, literally melts in your mouth. The clam flavor (and actual clam) is largely M.I.A., and N.O.'s cakes are twice as expensive as competitors', but if this isn't an argument for a fresh perspective on an old favorite, you can hand me another bag of Drum Rock.

The Quiet Company Behind So Many Southern New England Clam Cakes and Fritters

Headquarters for the business most responsible for the rise of clam cakes in Southern New England (literally and figuratively) is a non-descript building off a busy commercial street far from the water: In other words, it's nothing like the charming seaside shacks where most clam cake memories are made.

The company is Drum Rock Products, and it produces the best-selling mix to make clam cakes. This is not based on sales figures (which this privately owned business declines to disclose) but on the large number of Southern New England seafood restaurant owners who admit to using Drum Rock Clam Cake & Fritter Mix. Extrapolating from them, I would guess that at least half (and probably more) of commercial establishments in Connecticut, Rhode Island, and Massachusetts who serve clam cakes get a Drum Rock assist.

Is this intensely local dish in the midst of Drum Rock McDonaldization?

Drum Rock president Stephen Hinger denies it. He says their mix only provides the dry ingredients used to make clam cakes. How they come out also depends on the kind and grade of oil being used, the type and quality of the clams, how the wet and dry ingredients are mixed, how often the oil is changed, and what temperature they're cooked at, for how long. "There are just many factors to keep the cakes from being the same," he explains.

See page 154 for Hinger's take on some of the wrong decisions people make about these things. Obviously, he thinks using his mix is the right one because it saves on staff time and eliminates mistakes employees might make if they mixed the flour, leavening, and milk themselves and helps ensure that clam cakes at a particular stand be "uniform every time."

In fact, the company was created in answer to one clam shack owner's cry for help. Edward McCabe was a salesman for Procter & Gamble's shortening and fat division in 1950 when one of his Cape Cod, Massachusetts, restaurant customers asked if McCabe knew of a ready-made clam fritter mix. McCabe didn't but said he would ask around, then immediately began working to create such a product.

That restaurateur became his first customer, and soon, enough of McCabe's other fat customers had signed on for him to quit his P&G job and launch the company, named after a local Narragansett tribe landmark. His company logo featured an Indigenous man standing on a rock holding a bar of gold above the slogan, "Good as gold."

Hinger was one year out of college and about to be laid off from his landscaping job when he heard about a Drum Rock opening. He worked there for 11 years before buying the company from McCabe's son in 1993.

And that's how this onetime aspiring landscape architect became Southern New England's clam cake king.

Hinger smiles at the title but suggests it is better suited to founder McCabe, who used to compete in daily sales competitions with his salesmen.

"He was a *real* salesman. . . . Knowing his product was out there more than any other one—it's what he lived for."

Though reserved in manner, Hinger is also a salesman, with answers to almost every objection to buying his clam cake mix. "People will say, 'We don't have the time or space to make fritters.' And I'll say, 'Do you have space for one bowl?' Or we'll ask, 'Do you serve chowder with complimentary oyster crackers? Why not sell a chowder-and-clam-cake combo you could charge extra for?'"

Those who claim their restaurants are too high-end for frying are asked if they serve calamari. "That's frying," Hinger tells them before suggesting lobster or smoked salmon fritter possibilities.

Recalcitrant stand owners aside, the business "almost runs itself," Hinger offers. Manufacturing seems particularly straightforward. It starts with Hinger choosing "Clam Cake" on the dropdown menu of a keypad connected to a computer programmed with the weights for all the ingredients. Within moments, a huge bag of flour that is suspended from the ceiling and connected to a scale releases the proper amount of powder into an auger that moves it up to a giant mixer. The process repeats for the whey, the two leaveners, and the salt. Once all of these all-natural ingredients are blended, another auger brings them to a hopper that releases the mix into a filling machine in the packaging room below. There the clam cake bags are either sealed or sewn on by other machines with the help of half a dozen employees.

During the busy summer season, Drum Rock will make fritter mix multiple times a day to meet the demands of mainly New England restaurants. The company also makes one whole-wheat pancake and two fish breading mixes, including the best-selling all-purpose Fis-Chic Wonder, whose year-round national appeal makes it the company's best-seller.

"The biggest problem with this business is not finding customers or the work itself—it's finding employees to show up and do the work," Hinger volunteers.

Which is one reason Hinger is glad one of his daughters is now working with him. Allie Hinger worked school vacations at Drum Rock since she was a teen and has a business degree and five years of experience with national retailer TJ Maxx. She describes her current situation at Drum Rock as gradually "prying more of the business away from" her dad in anticipation of an eventual takeover.

She brought political correctness to the 73-year-old company by recently changing the Drum Rock logo from an Indigenous man to a toque-topped chef. "It needed to go," she insists, although no one complained, and the Drum Rock is reportedly a real historical thing. (See side story.)

On the other hand, the company has also not gotten any calls or posts from outraged Drum Rock Indian fans.

Drum Rock Field Trip

Drum Rock was actually two large rocks located in the Apponaug section of Warwick, Rhode Island, and balanced on one another, so as to make a loud drumming noise when rocked. Narragansett tribe members reportedly did this to send messages. But twentieth-century teenagers rocking the rock in the wee hours annoyed neighbors enough that the city government repositioned the rocks so they would no longer make noise.

You can still see the silenced landmark by taking an 8-minute drive from the Drum Rock Products building to the entrance of the parking lot for Cowesett Hills Apartment numbers 14, 15, and 16 (3595 Post Rd., Warwick, RI). Then walk across the street. The rock can be identified by the rectangular indent from the missing historic marker that once explained all of the above.

Some Places That Start with Drum Rock

Amaral's, Anthony's, Blount Clam Shacks, Captain Frosty's, Champlin's, Dune Brothers, Evelyn's, Jim's Dock, Kate's Seafood, Monahan's, Quito's, Sea Swirl, Rocky Point Clam Shack, Tony's, and Two Little Fish

Jelly Bean Fritters

State fairs are laboratories of weird fried foods. Drum Rock came up with this dessert adaptation of their fritter mix after hearing of the dish's debut at the Big E multi-state fair in Springfield, Massachusetts.

    2 cups Drum Rock Products Fritter & Clam Cake Mix

    ½ to ¾ cup water

    ½ cup jelly beans in two complementary flavors (lemon and lime, cinnamon and apple, or coconut and pineapple, for instance)

    1 tablespoon confectioners' or granulated sugar

Fill deep fryer with oil and heat to 350°F. Empty fritter mix into a large bowl and add ½ cup of water. Gently fold the water into the mix just until blended and not one stir more! (The mix should be thicker than pancake batter but not as firm as pie or cookie dough. Add more water, if necessary, to create that consistency.) Let stand 5 to 10 minutes. Scatter jelly beans into batter but do not stir them in. Grab batter and a few jelly beans with an ice cream scoop then carefully drop into the fryolator. Each fritter should take about 2 to 3 minutes to cook; you can fry them in batches, taking care to turn them over so they are golden brown all over and cooked thoroughly.

Remove fritters from oil. Then either place the fritters in a paper bag with the sugar and shake or put them on a plate and dust with sugar using a fine strainer. (Put sugar in strainer then tap its side while moving over the fritters.) Cool slightly before eating.

Yield: 16 to 24 fritters, serving 4 to 6

JIM'S DOCK
1175 SUCCOTASH RD., NARRAGANSETT, RI, 401-783-2050

There's a good reason this place is called Jim's Dock, rather than Jim's Clam Bar or Jim's Snack Shack and Restaurant.

This is primarily a place where people dock their boats. Lona Hoffman only sets out 8 tables and 23 chairs and serves food alongside the busy Galilee Channel as a summertime side business.

Food by Jim's; entertainment by the Galilee boating traffic

Jim's Dock was John's bait shop when Hoffman's grandfather, Jim DeCubellis, and his son, Dave, bought and renamed it in 1971. At some point, Dave's brother-in-law, Ray Lovejoy, started selling egg sandwiches and grinders to local fishermen. The menu expanded and evolved from there.

"I was peeling potatoes for home fries here when I was 10 years old," recalls Hoffman, now a third-generation owner. During the tuna fishing boom of the early to mid-1980s, she had to give up her bedroom to a couple of sushi experts who came over from Japan to grade and price the tuna before it was shipped to foreign markets.

But she also remembers swimming and crabbing off the docks and nearby beach with the neighborhood kids and her sibs, and perhaps most importantly, hanging with her dad, a state cop and ex-Marine who died in 2014. His accomplishments, including a Purple Heart, are all over the walls of the wooden building containing the restaurant's kitchen. "We spent all day every day here in the summer. It was a wonderful way to grow up," she says.

Hoffman still makes Jim's clam cakes the way her Uncle Ray taught her: folding in, rather than mixing, the Drum Rock mix with the other ingredients. "If you overwork it, the cakes will be too heavy," she says. She prefers them "smaller," by which she means baseball-sized, because larger ones "take longer to cook and end up being hard."

The words are hardly out of her mouth when a basket of softball-sized clam cakes arrives hot from the kitchen. "Kids!" she exclaims in exasperation with her new fryer chef, although the cakes don't seem hard as much as extra crispy. She estimates that 80 percent of her dinner customers order them, including curious tourists and most locals.

The small menu also includes cornflake-battered fried fluke and flounder, swordfish and mahi-mahi tacos, and scallops she gets direct from a former classmate-turned-fisherman. There's also usually at least one salad and grilled fish dish on special. Landlubbers can get a Saugy, Rhode Island's favorite natural-casing hot dog.

Like a lot of other restaurateurs, Hoffman struggled to find help during the pandemic. Unlike a lot of other casual ones, Jim's still has servers, albeit fewer than before.

"I used to have seven waitresses, now there's four. There used to be five in the kitchen, now there's three, including me. I'm here 11 a.m. to close."

Not that she's complaining.

"What could be better than being on the water all summer?" she asks, her deep tan providing the proof. "That's been my life, and I know I've been very, very lucky."

MACRAY'S SEAFOOD
115 STAFFORD RD., TIVERTON, RI, 401-625-1347,
MACRAYSSEAFOOD.COM

Two grass-topped Tiki Jack's mobile bars dominate the little strip mall on Stafford Road in Tiverton. Another big sign just behind them could lead you to believe this is just another Del's Lemonade store. (See side story.) It would be easy to miss that this is actually also—and mainly—the successor home of one of the South Coast of Massachusetts's most storied seafood shacks.

From the late 1940s until its 1986 closing, Macray's of nearby Westport, Massachusetts, was a legendary source of fried clams and clam cakes for ordinary eaters and famous foodies like Emeril Lagasse.

Current owner Mike Napolitano didn't know all this when he bought the business. It was just one of the more modest of a number of locations he looked at as a permanent home for his Tiki Jack's tropical food and drink catering concept. Seeing Macray's single takeout window and four-table dining room for the first time after Napolitano's 2018 purchase, "My wife cried," he admits.

Undeterred, Napolitano put in an oven and started offering baked cod and scallops as the beginning of a transition to a more contemporary seafood menu. At the same time, he started pursuing a Del's Lemonade franchise.

"I was planning to totally change the menu," Napolitano confesses. Until he saw how many customers were ordering Macray's old fried items, and Napolitano started realizing what he had.

Macray's Mike Napolitano and his crusty clam cakes

Today's Macray's is the evolution in Napolitano's thinking about his business made manifest. Is Macray's a tiki bar? A Del's franchise outlet? A seafood joint? It is, actually, a slightly confusing all-of-the-above. Owner-identified highlights from the wide-ranging menu include the lobster roll, baked seafood casserole, and Macray's-style fried clams and clam cakes (the latter obviously being what anyone reading this book should order).

"I like a little salt," Mike says as he puts a plate of the ungainly golden orbs on a high-top in his palm-tree-adorned parking lot patio, as if to head off a criticism he's heard before. They are, indeed, quite salty.

But what a fry! A better crust on a clam cake would be hard to find—great fried chicken would be more like it.

Napolitano got his fried fish recipes, including the clam cake one, from previous owner Bob Lafleur, who worked at the original stand for 13 years.

The new Macray's got best clam cakes in *South Coast Today*'s 2014 reader's poll. Even more important are the qualified endorsements from the original owners' kids.

"Decent," said Deborah Haskell, daughter of Macray's owner/chief clam cake maker Ed Haskell. "As close as you can get to the original" for a recipe that was never written down, says Tom McGreevy, son of the "Mac" in Macray's.

Macray's: The Origin Story

Food writer David Leite began his 2007 *New York Times* clam shack story with a memory of "digging into the red-and-white cardboard boxes" of fried clams at Macray's. "To eat at any place but Macray's was . . . familial treason when I was growing up," he concluded.

The *Boston Globe* once told of a South Coast fish-and-chip shop whose owner answered customers' demand for fried clams by posting a sign directing them to Macray's.

This is not to mention the frequent shout-outs Macray's has gotten on the Food Network from celebrity chef (and area native) Emeril Lagasse.

All this love for a 12-by-12-foot shack.

At first, it was a hot dog stand, its name a portmanteau of the names of owners Tom "Mac" McGreevy and Ray Therien. But soon the hot dogs were replaced by seafood and Therien by Mac's high school friend, Ed Haskell, and the lines grew.

The location—just down the street from Lincoln Park amusement park and not far from Horseneck Beach—helped. So did the partners' frugality about anything that didn't directly affect food quality.

"The building was crap," recalls Haskell's daughter, Deborah. The parking lot, not much better. "It was dirt and rocks, so when it rained, there were potholes that people had to drive around. People said, 'Jesus, why don't you guys pave this thing?' My father and Mac would say, 'Hey, if you don't want to come, don't come.'

"Still they came," Deborah continues, some parking illegally on the highway instead of the lot. "Every spring the town of Westport put up signs, 'No parking on the highway.' Every winter, the snow plows would knock them down. They did that little dance."

But when it came to kitchen equipment and food ingredients, "They bought the best of everything," says Deborah, who accompanied her father on food-buying trips as a kid. "Their clams were always fresh, and they came from one place: the Chesapeake Bay in Maryland, not Ipswich. They used lard: huge cubes that came in a box. And we went to a local farm to buy the eggs."

In the late 1960s or early 1970s, they discontinued fish and chips—one of their most popular dishes—when haddock got too expensive rather than replace it with a fish the partners considered inferior.

That left only four menu items: fried clams, French fries, clam cakes, and soda. Each food got its own deep fryer to "prevent the melding of flavors," Mac's son, Tom McGreevy, recalled.

By the time Bob Lafleur got a job cleaning Macray's parking lot in 1973, it was open summer weekends only. The partners were supporting their families for 365 days on only 24 days of sales, which should give you an idea of how busy they were. Lafleur remembers "lines of people stretching back to the highway" and he and his fellow employees, one of whom did nothing but pour soda, "sweating like pigs." Air conditioning was open doors and windows with no screens.

Mac and her dad "were like machines," Deborah Haskell says.

But eventually, even machines break down. When Mac and Ed quit, the place closed.

Until Lafleur, who was cooking at the end, got the late partners' families' blessing to open Macray's II. (With most other businesses this locally famous, this would have been handled by lawyers. But Haskell told him, "My dad would be proud. Go for it.")

The original property on Route 6 in Westport was too expensive when Lafleur went to do his 1996 reboot and is now a pile of rubble from a subsequent fire. But its legacy lives on in memories and the fryolators at Macray's in Tiverton. "We just had a birthday party here for a 95-year-old who remembers when," says current owner/happy beneficiary Mike Napolitano.

Del's All Over the Damn Place

It's hard to throw a beach ball in Southern New England without hitting a green-and-yellow sign of the snow-covered lemon that stands for Del's.

Though the frozen fruit treat was originally sold only at dedicated stands or roaming trucks, it's now on the menus of an increasing number of clam shacks (like Iggy's and Macray's), ice cream stands, convenience stores, sports venues, pushcarts—heck, I once saw a Del's raft serving swimmers off the state pier in Jerusalem.

Why so many Del's when essentially all they're selling is Italian ice, Americanized granita that you can buy at seasonal stands anywhere Italians settled in this country?

Del's started out similarly: In 1948, Angelo DeLucia began making lemon slush from his Neapolitan grandfather's recipe in a little hut under a shortened version of his last name. But then he opened additional stands and sent out trucks to blanket his small state of Rhode Island so early and completely that Italian ice is there known only as Del's or Del's Lemonade or frozen lemonade (after Del's original and still most popular flavor, though watermelon is gaining on it).

Another possible reason Del's rules Rhode Island: It's all-natural. The founding lemon flavor, for instance, is made only with water, sugar, and every part of the lemon but the stem. Del's is also different from convenience store Slurpees in how it's served: in a paper cup without straw or spoon. The Del's veteran repeatedly slurps and shakes as the finely chopped ice melts from the warmth of their hot little hand.

Speaking of hot: It's hard to imagine a more refreshing chaser to a fried fish dinner in the summer. If your clam cake place of choice doesn't serve Del's, consider making a trip to one of the original stands (in Cranston or Coventry) that defined the brand before Del's became ubiquitous.

MONAHAN'S CLAM SHACK BY THE SEA
190 OCEAN RD., NARRAGANSETT, RI, 401-782-2524,
MONAHANSRI.COM

Matthew Combs is living the dream—in more than one way.

1. He works only about half the year in one of the most beautiful waterfront settings imaginable.

2. "Own my own restaurant" was literally what he wrote when a teacher once asked Combs's class to commit their hopes and dreams to paper.

Combs is actually not the first person in his family to dream this dream.

Combs's grandfather, Joseph Monahan, and, later, uncle Michael had run a gas station, bait shop, and, eventually, seafood shack on this same oceanside spot since the 1940s. That explains the souvenir T-shirt Monahan's sells bearing the original Monahan's Cove bait shop name.

Michael Monahan leased the shack to a couple who ran it as the Starboard Galley for about a decade before Michael died and left the place to Combs, his two siblings, and a cousin. Being the one with "the dream" and some restaurant work experience, Combs was the natural one to run it.

For the most part, Combs has kept the simple, traditional Rhode Island summer shack menu of fish, burgers, and dogs that he found when he took over. Chowder and clam cakes (made with Drum Rock mix) remain bestsellers. Combs believes it's because "they have such a short window. It's almost like apple cider donuts in the fall: People know they can get clam cakes in the summer and, for the most part, only in the summer. It's anticipated, and people want their fix."

On-trend dishes that Combs has introduced include a grilled swordfish taco with basil pesto and pico de gallo and a local flounder fried fish sandwich with mango-peach salsa and chipotle aioli.

Add that to the stand's drop-dead gorgeous perch on the Narragansett sea wall and a sunny summer Saturday and you might be among more than a hundred people standing in line to eat here.

Still, Monahan's seems noticeably more chill than many of its similarly slammed counterparts.

Combs credits a young staff that returns summer after summer and so know what they're doing, rather than his own easy-going personality, though that also probably helps. So does Combs's instinct to act less like an owner and more like a coach or teacher.

Among those working in his tiny kitchen are five of the seven members of the fourth generation of this Monahan family business, one of whom, Combs hopes, will share his dream of owning their own restaurant—at some point not very soon.

QUITO'S RESTAURANT
411 THAMES ST., BRISTOL, RI, 401-253-4500,
QUITOSRESTAURANT.COM

Clam cakes are infamously full of fat and calories. But this is not of great concern for the many people who discover clam cake maker Quito's at the end of the popular Providence-to-Bristol East Bay Bike Path. For them, the cakes are an earned reward for calories they've already worked off—or welcome fuel for the 14 miles back.

Quito's is located right on the water because it was originally a fish market. Eight years after their 1954 opening, Peter and JoAnne Quito put a few picnic tables out and started selling fish and chips. Clam cakes were added in 1975.

At first glance from the parking lot circling the waterfront park in front of the building, Quito's still looks like a tiny little fish market/clam shack. You have to get a lot closer to see all the extra outdoor seating the Quitos' son, current owner Al Quito, currently in his late sixties, added after the bike path was completed in the early 1990s.

Although Al's parents are now gone, the place remains a family affair, with Al now running it with son Michael and daughter Alyssa.

The twenty-first-century Quito's has two identities: daytime takeout restaurant for the bikers and full-service, sit-down one for locals and summer visitors who come to have cocktails and dinner while watching the sun set over the water.

Lobster rolls, chowder, and clam cakes are the best-sellers with both groups. The cakes are ping-pong-ball-sized and dense, a product of Drum Rock mix doctored with white pepper and "a special clam juice" that offers a more consistently superior flavor than the fresh chopped sea clams these also contain, Al believes. "We also put in a lot of clams—people say, 'You actually have clams in them!'" Al says.

Although their old wooden roadside sign suggests otherwise, Quito's is no longer a fish market. But Al says he keeps his father's dealer's license so he can still buy some fish directly from local fishermen—mostly shellfish like quahogs, mussels, and lobster.

Quito's also has a full bar and soft drinks with 100 percent cane sugar in old-fashioned flavors like birch and spruce beer, cream, and sarsaparilla from the over 90-year-old Bristol bottler Empire.

For years, Al shared cooking duties with business partner Frank Formisano: Al handled the lobster rolls and fried items while Formisano prepared the Italian seafood pasta and baked dishes. "When he left, I started doing it all. I surprised myself at how good those dishes were," says Al.

So good that some local supermarkets are carrying jarred versions of the zuppa and Mediterranean sauces he makes at the restaurant, in case you're wondering what else to order besides the clam cakes.

ROCKY POINT CLAM SHACK
SOMEWHERE IN THE WEST BAY AREA OF RHODE ISLAND,
401-738-9830, ROCKYPOINTCLAMSHACK.WEEBLY.COM

If Rocky Point's Shore Dinner Hall hadn't been torn down in 2014 and people were still selling clam cakes and chowder out of the decaying building, it might look something like Rocky Point Clam Shack.

It consists of a couple of once brightly colored—now faded—conjoined trailers decorated with all manner of Rocky Point amusement park memorabilia pumping out dinner hall favorites like chowder and clam cakes in a parking lot 6 miles from the original Rocky Point. Place your order beside the haunted house stuffed mannequin at the first trailer and pick it up under the Rocky-the-Lobster-adorned front gate look-alike at the next.

At least, that's how it was until June 2022, when their Route 1, Warwick location's new owner didn't renew their lease—though they do plan to reopen somewhere nearby in summer 2023.

The shack opened in 2014 as a tribute to the late beloved local institution by someone who owes his very existence to it: Rocky Point Shack founder Anthony Restivo's parents met at the amusement park. More than just a sea-food shack, Rocky Point Clam Shack was intended to be a living history museum where people could eat facsimiles of the park's food while gazing adoringly at the aforementioned Rocky, the circa 1967 Leo the Lion statue, and the parking sign from the park's Palladium/Windjammer event facilities, among other items Restivo bought after the park went under.

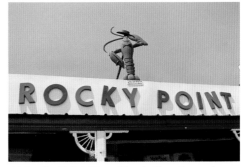

At Rocky Point Clam Shack, the clam cakes come with a large side of nostalgia.

There were problems from the start: the reproduction placemats and original ride ticket table decor that walked; the falling out between Restivo and investor partner Ping Hou that saw Restivo exit, leaving a skeleton crew of three to battle with the dual demands of making food and maintaining historical objects. In 2021, the food was winning. A trash can rests in the middle of the replica zoo. A row of children's rides sits idle under yellow police tape.

The shack still has its charms, chief among them garrulous assistant manager and chef Rick Roden, who injects some of the namesake park's fun into lunch by bribing fish-adverse kids to try clam cakes with money out of his own pocket and getting on the loudspeaker to solicit applause for brave clam cake first-timers.

Roden met Hou trying to sell him promotional refrigerator magnets just before Roden got into a serious motorcycle accident. Hou brought a lobster roll and some chowder to the hospital. "Now I'm his consigliore—I do whatever he needs," Roden says.

That includes nursing clam cakes out of the shack's antique donut-making machine. One day early that season, its metal arm gave way, the funnel holding all the batter fell into the fryer, and Roden had to make an emergency run to Home Depot for a replacement bolt.

"Rule number one for working here? Do not run out of clam cakes." Rule number two: Expect "a lot of people lecturing you about Rocky Point's clam cakes and chowder," Roden says.

Some people tell him they used to be bigger than the shack's 50-cent-sized ones. But Roden worked at the park for three summers when he was young and remembers differently. Plus, "The bigger they are the longer they have to cook, the longer they're in the oil, which can make them greasy."

Roden's method for checking doneness is as old-school as his equipment.

"You want it to be a glowing bright orange or just past that to an autumnal color. That's your perfect clam cake," he says.

The shack packages these "perfect" cakes in Chinese takeout cartons—10 to 13 per box—though Roden longs for the paper sacks used at Rocky Point—and still at some other places—that allow you to "sprinkle some salt and pepper on top, close it up, and shake," he recalls dreamily.

There's no question that much of Rocky Point Clam Shack's business is driven by this kind of park nostalgia. On the other hand, as Roden points out, "For a lot of younger people, Rocky Point is this place."

TWO LITTLE FISH
300 ATLANTIC AVE., WESTERLY, RI, 401-348-9941

Two Little Fish is a seafood shack that doubles as an ecology class. Far outnumbering the signs of instruction that quietly boss you around at most takeouts are posters, display panels, and even videos about the evils of plastic six-pack rings ("No rings at Two Little Fish except onion!"), funding of sea animal rescues (partially by your purchase), and their bucket-for-bucks deal (fill a sand pail with trash from the beach across the street and get $1 off your meal).

Where other stands use their menus to rhapsodize about Great Aunt Emma's amazing fritter recipe, Two Little Fish instead boasts of fresh seafood that is "wild caught (never farmed) and sustainable (not from an endangered fish stock)," all served on compostable plates with plant-fiber utensils.

It would be annoying if the food wasn't so good—they've won best seafood in the local newspaper's reader's poll every year since 2007. And if owner Tim Brennan (i.e., One Fish) wasn't so friendly and forthright in admitting that he and co-owner Kevin Urbonas (Two Fish, and Brennan's brother-in-law) weren't always such eco-saints.

"Hurricane Sandy was a wake-up call," says Brennan. Two Little Fish had just wrapped up its first season in a new location sandwiched between Misquamicut Beach and Winnapaug Salt Pond when Sandy struck, driving the restaurant across the street under their deck.

Brennan and Urbonas's restaurant had previously been located on safe, inland Granite Street, but the upbeat Brennan won't take the bait to talk about bad timing.

"We actually were lucky—at least we had our four walls. . . . But it got us thinking about how this happened and gave us a major push in the direction of sustainable dining," he says between delivering orders and chatting up customers in the small indoor dining room.

Brennan acquired his seafood shack chops during a 14-year career at Lenny & Joe's, a well-respected seafood place in Madison, Connecticut. In fact, in 1997, Two Little Fish launched as a branch of Lenny & Joe's. Five years in, Brennan and Urbonas decided to strike out on their own as "Two Little Fish" in a big seafood restaurant pond.

Clam cakes are not as common in Connecticut and were not on Lenny & Joe's menu or on Brennan and Urbonas's radar until a customer explained how they were missing the boat on this RI seafood favorite.

"I went online to see what he was talking about," Brennan admits sheepishly. And he's glad he did. Their clam fritters are now their third most popular item behind fish and chips and lobster rolls (Connecticut nomenclature for them notwithstanding). The crispy, golden, ping-pong-ball-sized orbs won the Clamarati's 2022 tasting contest and "are an add-on to almost every order," says Brennan.

Getting up to speed on seafood ecology and sustainable restaurant practices took a while longer.

The first order of eco-business was getting rid of plastic bags and bottles and foam containers. Says Brennan: "Most plastic never breaks down. It eventually ends up in the water and your fried clams and clam fritters."

It's not an image likely to drive clam sales. But this place has bigger fish to fry than money. Otherwise Two Little Fish would sell their used cooking oil instead of giving it away to Newport Biodiesel as part of a program that provides heat and gas to local needy families.

Going green has pushed Two Little Fish's costs up significantly. But that increase has been more than covered by an influx of new, eco-conscious guests. Says Brennan: "People are as hungry for socially responsible businesses as they are for fried seafood."

Psycho Seagulls on the Patio

Know who loves clam cakes as much as you? Seagulls. They much prefer fried seafood and fries to their natural diet of raw clams, insects, and small animals, and who can blame them? But it's problematic for seaside seafood shacks with outdoor seating.

This is an especially big challenge for Two Little Fish and Iggy's in Rhode Island and the Lobster Shack at Two Lights in Maine, if the number of signs on their properties warning people about the seagulls is any clue.

Tim Brennan of Two Little Fish says gulls have plucked lobster rolls and hamburgers right out of his customers' hands. He considers their replacement "part of the cost of doing business."

Their known klepto MO notwithstanding, gulls are a protected species. Blame the seascape painting lobby! So clam shack owners have limited power.

"I have a thing on the roof that makes noise [to scare them away]," says Iggy's owner David Gravino. "It helped for a short time. I also tried a decoy owl [a predator], but the seagulls just sit right next to it. They know it's fake."

Gravino has yet to put spikes on the roof to discourage seagull loitering and probably won't. "Seagulls are part of our family," he says with a shrug of surrender.

What's a fan of outdoor dining to do? Take one or more of the following defensive actions.

- Never voluntarily feed seagulls human food. This started the problem and perpetuates it.

- Keep food hidden and covered while walking from the takeout window to your seat. Protect your ice cream cone like it was a newborn.

- Look up for gulls perched on posts, walls, and buildings above and around the patio area before sitting down. Try to choose a seat far away from them against a wall so you can anticipate and avert an attack.

- Save gesticulating while talking for indoor venues. Certainly don't do it while holding food: To a gull, that's an offering.

- Forgot the catsup or utensils? Don't abandon your food to get it: It might not be there when you get back.

- Gull looks like it's about to attack? Try making eye contact and staring him down. This often works for human pickpockets and, in one 2019 English study, deterred almost a third of opportunistic seagulls.

Gulls can be big and scary-looking, especially when they're swooping in on you. But, ornithologists say, it's food and not you that they're after. Unless they think you're threatening their babies.

And, unfortunately, gull nesting season pretty much coincides with the clam shack one.

>> If you don't want to fight the seagulls at Two Little Fish, drive four minutes east on Atlantic Avenue to the hyper-casual **Salty's** (668 Atlantic Ave., Westerly, RI, 401-322-8219, facebook.com/seawellseafood), owned by local wholesale seafood distributor Sea Well and helmed by chef Charlie Atkinson, a veteran of a number of fine dining restaurants in Texas. Yes, apparently, there are some. But no, this does not mean clam fritters with barbecue dipping sauce but rather a unique blend of sea clams (for texture) and quahogs (for flavor) in these crunchy Drum Rock-based cakes.

YE OLDE ENGLISH FISH & CHIPS
25 S. MAIN ST., WOONSOCKET, RI, 401-762-3637,
YEOLDEENGLISHFISHANDCHIPS.COM

The name should give you a clue to the must-order. The Robinson family has been selling authentic batter-style English fish and chips in this northern Rhode Island mill town for more than a hundred years.

The Ye Olde English Fish & Chips crew in all their red-uniformed splendor in the late 1970s. Three generations of Robinson owners are pictured: grandfather Harry with wife Mae (extreme right), father Gordon (center) with wife Elaine (to his left), and Steve (above right of Gordon).

They've only been making clam cakes since 2015. And yet the first and biggest sign people see upon entering the building today is for their $6.25 clam cakes and chowder special.

That's because, owner Steven Robinson explains, clam cakes are the menu item that now fills fish and chip's former role as "poor man's food."

Ye Olde's fish and chips are still made from the recipe Robinson's great-grandfather Harry Sowden learned while working in a fish-and-chip shop in his native England; since 1932, in this Tudor-style former home of the local English-American society with ye olde black-and-white tile floor.

You might think that fellow English émigrés made Ye Olde a success, but you'd be wrong. It was actually French Canadians who came to work in the city's textile mills in large numbers at the turn of the twentieth century. They ate fish as a way to meet their Catholic religion's prohibitions against eating meat on Fridays and during Lent without going broke.

One recent Friday, Robinson showed off a second kitchen that was built in the 1970s mainly to fulfill large mill orders. Although most of the mills and many of the French Canadians' and Catholic dietary restrictions are now gone, the restaurant is still busiest on Fridays and during Lent. (File this under the category of old habits die hard.)

Clam cakes are part of a seafood menu expansion that started with fried fish sandwiches in the 1960s and now includes fried clams, shrimp, and scallops. In addition to being affordable, Robinson says the cakes go great with Ye Olde's Manhattan red clam and extra-creamy white seafood chowders—themselves so popular that on Fridays they're dished up from their own chowder bar.

Ye Olde uses either Drum Rock or the corn-containing Krisppe mixes interchangeably to make the cakes. Mix price and availability are the deciding factors—Robinson says neither he nor his customers notice much of a difference.

But Robinson does feel strongly about his frying oil: He uses a meat-vegetable (MV) oil blend exclusively. All-vegetable oil can't match its flavor and color, he insists. His grandfather used 100 percent lard rendered from meat on-site.

"It used to smell like prime rib in here," recalls Robinson, who started peeling potatoes for French fries when he was 15 and now runs the place with sister Diane Durand. (Ye Olde still makes their own French fries, though they're now peeled by machine.)

The other dish for cheapskates is fish cake. This is not the pan-fried fish-and-mashed-potato patties of early New England but rather an authentic English version of similar frugality consisting of odd pieces of white fish sandwiched between two slices of potato that is dipped in thick batter and fried. The only original menu item besides fish and chips, it typically sells out by late afternoon on Fridays, it's so popular.

Other old-time oddities include dill pickles ($1) and York Peppermint Patties (also $1), the dark-chocolate-covered peppermint cream candy from an era when having fish or garlic breath was considered uncouth. "It takes away the fish aftertaste," Robinson explains.

"And if we don't have them, we hear about it," added one eavesdropping counter worker.

The history of Ye Olde English is not just on its menu but also in pictures and newspaper articles posted all over the restaurant's wood-paneled walls.

Robinson is respectful but not sentimental about his family's legacy business. For instance, Ye Olde's May 2022 100th anniversary celebration consisted not of a party but instead of $10.00 and $19.22 combo meal specials.

Rhode Island Surf and Turf

Before you place an outsized order at Ye Olde English Fish & Chips, you should know that you are just around the corner from New York Lunch, another century-plus-old business specializing in another low-brow, bad-for-you food specialty that is (name notwithstanding) unique to Rhode Island. We are talking about New York System wieners.

Order one of these wieners "all the way" (which is really the *only* way) and you'll get a pale little hot dog in a steamed bun topped with raw onion, mustard, celery salt, and a meat sauce full of the warm spices used by the Greek-Americans who invented this dish and still serve it at diners and lunch counters all over the state (including ones near Dune Brothers in Providence and Blount's and Amaral's in Warren).

Rhode Island New York System wieners are close cousins to the Coney Island wieners popular in the Midwest and have the same tenuous connection to New York: Coney Island was the first place beef sausages were sold as sandwiches, and immigrants who fanned out from Ellis Island to sell hot dogs around the country in the early 1900s wanted to make it clear they were selling the same thing.

Except that they weren't really: There is no history of putting chili sauce on hot dogs at Coney Island and no tradition of the sausages being all-beef in Rhode Island the way they were at Nathan's Famous and other New York stands serving pork-averse Jewish customers.

In fact, Rhode Island hot wieners are more like oversized Vienna sausages, a four-inch mystery mix of minced pork, beef, veal, and/or chicken. Like White Castle hamburgers—their brothers in grease and affordability—New York System hot wieners are ordered in multiples, even by the daintiest eaters, and are a time-honored nightcap to a night of drinking.

As for the "system" in New York System: It refers to the way the dish is traditionally made, which is with the buns rolled out on somebody's arm like piano keys and filled at lightning speed. Today's Rhode Island Health Department supposedly frowns on this, though a photo of an employee's bare, bun-covered arm was prominently displayed on one wiener joint's 2022 web page.

Beaches Near the Cakes In Rhode Island

South County (along the shoreline from Westerly to Narragansett)

Where the greatest number of great clam cake joints and the best sandy beaches meet. Fees are parking for nonresidents in the summer. Nonresident parking fee at all RI state beaches except Misquamicut is $12/$14 weekdays/weekends.

Charlestown Breachway, 812–774 Charlestown Beach Rd., Charlestown. Calm-water swimming and saltwater fishing.

East Beach State Beach, East Beach Rd., Charlestown. Probably the most unspoiled beach in Rhode Island. But beware of its riptides and very small parking lot.

East Beach, off Bluff Ave., Westerly. Not to be confused with the state beach of the same name, this one is known for its proximity to greatness (i.e., Taylor Swift, who has a Watch Hill beach home and has frolicked here with her famous friends). No lifeguards or parking lot: You need to find legal street parking and one of the right-of-way paths to access the beach.

East Matunuck State Beach, 950 Succotash Rd., South Kingstown. As with most popular state beaches, arrive before 9 a.m. or after 1 p.m. or forget it. Notoriously strong surf.

Misquamicut State Beach, 257 Atlantic Ave., Westerly. First and favorite RI beach stop for many Nutmeggers and New Yorkers. $20/$30 weekdays/weekends.

Salty Brine State Beach, 254 Great Island Rd., Galilee. Small, protected beach with a front-row seat on the ferries and fishing boats coming in and out of the channel. Limited parking.

Narragansett Town Beach, 39 Boston Neck Rd., Narragansett. One of few RI beaches that charge for admission and parking (although there is some free but timed parking along the sea wall). Adjacent to Monahan's. Some people just come to watch the surfers. $12/person plus $10/$15 weekdays/weekends for parking.

Scarborough State Beach, off Ocean Ave., Narragansett. Huge and hugely popular with teens and people from mid-Rhode Island cities, this place has plenty of parking and is great for people watching (but can get rowdy).

Roger W. Wheeler State Beach, 100 Sand Hill Cove Rd., Narragansett. Adjacent and similar to Salty Brine's in being toddler friendly but with lots more parking.

East Bay

Rocky Point State Park, 3275 Post Rd., Warwick. See full write-up on p. 5.

Oakland Beach, Oakland Beach Ave., Warwick. Urban beach on a saltwater inlet. Lots of restaurants are nearby, including Iggy's. Also popular for fishing. $12/$14 weekdays/weekends.

Coarser sand than South County beaches.

Bristol Town Beach, 50 Asylum Rd., Bristol. Rocky beach and a sports complex for the kids. $10/$20 weekdays/weekends.

Easton's Beach (aka First Beach), 175 Memorial Blvd., Newport. Across the street from Flo's. Oceanside surfing beach with carnival-like attractions. Free, famed Cliff Walk of ocean views and historic mansions begin here. $15/$25 weekdays/weekends.

Fogland Beach, 12 Point View Dr., Tiverton. A black stone beach with a nature preserve on the Sakonnet River. Great views, windsurfing, and kayaking. $10/$20 weekdays/weekends.

Grimmell's Beach (aka Island Park Beach), 428–366 Park Ave., Portsmouth. Rocky beach on the Sakonnet River across from Flo's Drive-In and Schultzy's. Free, including some free street parking.

Grinnell's Beach, 1860 Main Rd., Tiverton. Small, family-oriented town beach on the Sakonnet. $10/$20 weekdays/weekends.

Second Beach (aka Sachuest), 474 Sachuest Point Rd., Middletown. Another ocean beach. $20/$30 weekdays/weekends.

Third Beach, Third Beach Rd., Middletown. Located at the mouth of the Sakonnet River and much calmer than First or Second. $20/$30 weekdays/weekends.

Warren Town Beach, 533 Water St., Warren. Family-friendly beach with shallow water, a playground, and sandy and grassy areas to spread out. $10/$20 weekdays/weekends.

CONNECTICUT

DEARY BROTHERS MIKE'S STAND
12 INTERVALE ST., PUTNAM, CT, 860-928-1191,
DEARYBROSMIKESSTAND.COM

The pandemic wiped out almost 100,000 US restaurants. But Deary Brothers Mike's Stand's business grew during that scary time.

How is that possible?

"It's my personality," explains dairy bar owner Mike Deary only partly in jest as he runs in and out of the kitchen to chat it up with suppliers, customers, and fans.

"Wonderful as always," one customer tells him when asked about her lunch.

"You look great, but you know my eyesight is not that good," he kids another.

Although he later admits that 80 years of experience with the takeout format so pivotal to pandemic restaurant success undoubtedly helped.

The seasonal stand was a "hobby" for this high school teacher, now retired with a pension. But still, he keeps showing up.

"It's a happy place," he explains, with a shrug. "How else would I get to see all these people? I might not know their names, but I know what they like to eat and whether they root for the Yankees or the Red Sox."

The stand is the sole survivor of a Deary family dairy business that once delivered milk to homes in a wide swath of Southeastern New England and ran convenience stores and half a dozen restaurants or dairy stands like this one.

Working the family business was a Deary tradition for Mike and his 12 siblings growing up that continues with the next generation and ensures staffing at a time when other restaurants struggle to get help.

It also secures the future: Two of Mike's 78 nieces and nephews—Gene and Evan Deary—are either the heirs apparent or, as Mike states at one point, have owned the business for the past five years. In a conversation about the stand with Gene present, Mike does almost all the talking. Asked who really is the owner, Evan says, "It's a slow process. Mike is a celebrity." Not to mention in the stand's name.

Large clam cake orders are no problem for Deary Brothers' enthusiastic Evan Deary.

Initially the stands only sold Deary ice cream. Hot dogs and hamburgers were added in the early 1960s and then, eventually, the fried fish dishes for which they are now known.

"At first the fish was frozen, but now we use fresh fish and clams, hand form our burger patties, cut our own chicken," and fry in oil that is changed daily. "You can tell the difference," Mike says. The clam cakes are also house-made. The recipe is from Mrs. Flarity, an employee at the family's long-shuttered Danielson stand, whose first name has been lost to time.

The cakes are lighter than most and have a wonderful fry. Their devoted following has included a man (now unrelatedly deceased) who would buy six dozen at the end of the season to freeze and reheat on major holidays and the admiring dairy stand competitor who clued us in.

Nestled in a grove of trees two buildings in from Route 12, a road that itself has long since been bypassed by Interstate 395, and nowhere near the water, Deary's is not a place a clam cake lover would likely find on their own.

Deary's is what this book is all about.

HANK'S DAIRY BAR
1006 NORWICH RD., PLAINFIELD, CT 860-564-2298,
HANKSDAIRYBAR.COM

Most dairy bar owners are okay with doling out generic soft-serve sundaes and cones and then calling it a summer.

Hank's has higher aspirations.

They're spelled out in a 200-word "mission statement" posted on the side of their white-clapboard building for all to see and judge them by. Some highlights:

"We will obtain top quality products and prepare them fresh daily."

"We will . . . use . . . decades old recipes" that "we have prided ourselves in for over 60 years."

"We will continue to give young people their first jobs" . . . making "their first work experience memorable with lasting, lifelong lessons."

Originally, Hank's only sold ice cream.

"We will give back to the community. We will make Hank's a favorite gathering spot."

A recent visit found the Plainfield institution to be on-mission.

Speaking to the first few points: Hank's makes an extraordinary number of from-scratch dishes for a tiny takeout, including hand-cut and breaded onion rings, their own chili, taco meat, New England clam chowder and tartar sauce, and signature clam cakes and peppery coleslaw.

The clam cakes are their best-selling fried item after French fries. They make six bowls every morning, yielding 500 clam cakes each, and stir up an additional six to nine bowls on busy days.

"Not your Rhode Island fritters," the menu proclaims. Meaning no offense to Rhode Islanders, owner Colleen Champagne says quickly. "But ours are lighter and airier, and not as cakey as ones at the Rhode Island shore."

Indeed, the outer fry is soft and delicate—reminiscent of good fried chicken—and the moist cake tastes of black pepper and onion. Like many of the best clam cakes, theirs are fried in beef fat—though co-owner Dane Wilde bemoans how hard it is becoming to get.

They're also smaller than the Rhode Island standard: ping-pong rather than tennis-ball-sized. To make up for it, a half-dozen order will actually get you 10; a dozen, 18 to 20—a nice surprise for all but parents trying to teach their kids to count.

When Hank Zurowski erected the now-retro-looking Dairy Bar building and sign next to his father-in-law's car dealership in 1957, it was just to sell ice cream. Champagne says Hank's was the first business in Connecticut to use Taylor's soft-serve ice-cream-making machine, and that he and his wife, Alice, were featured in early ads for that company. (Hank's now uses a newer Taylor machine, fed with hand-flavored Hood strawberry and coffee ice cream in addition to the standard premade chocolate, vanilla, and twist, in yet another example of the owners' extra effort.)

Hamburgers and hot dogs were added in 1958 and clams with bellies and clam cakes by the early 1960s. Champagne and Wilde were both 16 when they were hired by Hank's sons, Scott and Pete. Both went off to do other things before circling back after, in Wilde's case, being laid off from Electric Boat, and, in Champagne's, graduating from college into a recession.

Champagne admits to not liking Wilde initially: "I was one of those girls who thought, 'If you can't do it perfectly, it shouldn't be done.' And he was the typical teenage boy"—leaving you to figure out what that means. But familiarity means, "We know what buttons not to push." Clear lines of responsibility also help: He does most of the prep work and cooking; she does the books and front of house, including training kids just like they used to be (yet another mission point, for those keeping score).

As for Hank's role as "gathering spot": Customers eat at a side area resembling a well-manicured public park, with picnic tables, swings for the kids, and a little shed with arcade games that doubles as a stage for free summer concerts. There's also the occasional parking lot car show and Polly the parrot, a Hank-era kiddy ride that still costs a quarter.

Keeping watch over all this from the ranch house on the rise behind the stand is one of the original architects of Hank's mission statement, Hank's son, Pete—sure to notice and say something should they ever stray.

JOHNNY AD'S
910 BOSTON POST RD., OLD SAYBROOK, CT, 860-388-4032, JOHNNYADS.COM

Can a Tibetan couple find success running a classic 1950s American drive-in restaurant on the WASPY Connecticut shoreline?

They apparently can because Johnny Ad's is omnipresent on lists of best lobster rolls and fresh fried fish in that state, as well as (even more importantly to the author of *The Great Clam Cake and Fritter Guide*) one of very few places a Nutmegger can get authentic and delicious Rhode Island clam chowder and clam fritters when the snow's flying.

Mailman Johnny Adinolfo opened this takeout shack in 1957 as a seasonal sideline with a classic drive-in menu of hamburgers, hot dogs, and shakes, only later adding the fried seafood for which it is now famed. (Although

Old Saybrook is on Long Island Sound, Johnny Ad's is on busy Route 1 rather than the water.)

Johnny Ad's son, also named Johnny, and his wife, Hildegard, took over in the early 1970s until, looking to move to Florida, they reluctantly sold it to Bob Hansen in 1995.

Reluctantly because the Adinolfos deemed Hansen's decades of experience managing high-end restaurants and hotels for

The stand was named for and by founder Johnny Adinolfo.

big corporations not relevant. It's only when their deal with a diner owner fell through that they agreed to meet with Hansen. It didn't help that he showed up for the meeting directly from a hotel convention wearing a business suit. Even today, Hansen's dress and courtly manner seem more suited to a country club than a clam shack.

The Adinolfos made the eventual deal contingent on Hansen's wife, Kathleen, working with him so that Johnny Ad's would keep its family feel. "It's not something we'd ever done before. We almost got a divorce!" Hansen says. Hansen's request that the Adinolfos stay on to show him the ropes also didn't work out too well. "After two weeks of them screaming at me, I let them go."

The Adinolfos lived right across the street and so, while still on Hansen's payroll, "sat on their porch staring at me and telling everyone—with glee—that I was not going to make it."

Why the animosity?

"It was probably because I put in an oven for baked and broiled dishes. I wanted to make it something nicer"—more like the restaurants he had managed before. And being from Michigan, "I didn't even really know what a clam shack was." Certainly not the way he does now, with a PA playing 1950s music between the calling-out of order numbers.

What Hansen did appreciate were the Adinolfos' "standards of quality and cleanliness" and commitment to from-scratch, made-to-order cooking that he maintains to this day. High school student workers peeled potatoes for chowder between filling orders one recent July evening.

The clam fritters are made from Johnny Ad's own recipe (including egg, sugar, lemon, and seasoned flour), instead of a commercial mix, which is probably why they have a crisper coating and more clams (and salt) than competitors'.

The stand is also known for lobster rolls served on grilled and buttered hot dog buns dressed with yet more butter (as per Connecticut custom) and fried clams and scallops, but also landlubber fare like foot-long hot dogs topped with stand-made chili.

Hansen says this is fortunate because the cost of clams and lobster has recently been so high that "we've had to accept less profit on them. It's the mix of seafood and non-seafood sales that keep us open."

And also the hard work of the Tibetan couple mentioned at the beginning of this story. When Tenzin Lama applied to work at Johnny Ad's as a recent émigré from Nepal in 1996, he knew even less about New England clam shacks than Hansen had when he bought Johnny Ad's. But Lama and his wife, Tsultim, have done such a good job managing the stand that, in 2000, Hansen made them co-owners.

Though their coming did put an end to Hansen's plan to add boiled lobster and steamers to Johnny Ad's menu.

Hansen had already spent a few thousand dollars on steaming equipment when his Buddhist partners informed him "in no uncertain terms that they would not be killing any animals for the business," Hansen recalls sheepishly.

THE LOBSTER SHACK
3 COSEY BEACH AVE., EAST HAVEN, CT, 203-483-8414,
LOBSTERSHACKCT.COM

The Lobster Shack is a big, beautiful sprawling complex of decks and dining rooms overlooking the water on three sides. The only thing shack-like about it is the seasonal schedule, self-serve format, and small menu of three chowders, one appetizer (I'm sure you can guess what), and nine sandwiches, three of them variations on their signature lobster roll.

How to explain this apparent mismatch? With a little history.

Nick Crismale was a Branford, Connecticut, fisherman who sold some of his lobster and clam catch out of a local marina. One day, he bought a small food trailer with the idea of setting up his 20-year-old daughter in a summer job selling hot dogs. But Alicia had other ideas for her school vacations, and the trailer just sat in the marina until Crismale told his wife, Arlene, he was going to sell it.

Ex-fisherman Nick Crismale with his flavorful clam fritters

That's when Arlene shared that she'd been thinking of using it to sell lobster rolls made with his lobster, recalled Crismale at one of the tables in his restaurant recently, looking every bit the weather-beaten fisherman he once was.

In the beginning, it was just something Arlene and a friend did for "fun"—the trailer was only big enough for two workers and had no name. Arlene eventually just followed the lead of customers in calling it "The Shack." Then media mentions started rolling in, culminating with a 2017 BuzzFeed piece saying they had the eleventh-best lobster roll in the country, and "the whole business exploded," Crismale recalls.

At first, Crismale just bought Arlene a bigger trailer, and when that too became too small, a former seafood restaurant one town over with room to grow "so we don't have to move again," he explains.

The new space was a boon for Connecticut clam fritter lovers: With its large kitchen, Crismale finally had room for a deep fryer. "I got [clam fritters] when I went to restaurants in Rhode Island, and I liked them. But being a clam fisherman, I couldn't help but notice that they didn't have any clams."

Or much flavor of any kind. "Traditionally, people dip the fritter in clam chowder, which gives them some taste and moistness. I wanted something that was more of a stand-alone appetizer."

Crismale experimented with a number of recipes before settling on an unusual one by Southern New England clam shack standards: It features orange, yellow, and green sweet peppers, Creole seasoning, garlic, chive, and beer, as well as the more traditional flour, eggs, clam juice, and baking powder, and lots of chopped, fresh quahog. The resulting fritter has a big crunch and bold garlic and clam flavors with an endnote of heat from the Creole seasoning and chipotle-mayo sauce side.

The Shack's Rhode Island-style clear clam chowder is also made on premises by Crismale, also with fresh quahogs, and was named "Best Rhode Island Clam Chowder in Connecticut" by a Connecticut newspaper (for what *that's* worth). The Lobster Shack sells 24 gallons a week.

The quahogs are no longer Nick's: He sold off his four-boat fleet and 5,000 acres of clam beds in 2015.

But doesn't his commercial fishing background give him an edge in buying?

A less straightforward person would just say yes. But Crismale says his best information on sourcing nowadays comes from customers.

"If you're not getting good fish, they let you know pretty quick," he says.

SEA SWIRL
30 WILLIAMS AVE., MYSTIC, CT, 860-536-3452,
SEASWIRLOFMYSTIC.COM

It's not uncommon for a seasonal New England ice cream stand to expand its menu into seafood. People are already there for dessert: Why not cash in on dinner too?

But few make that leap with the seriousness and success of the Sea Swirl. None of their seafood is frozen. Employees pick the beards off their clams by hand and shuck and chop fresh quahogs for their clam chowder. The non-seafood side of the menu includes homemade chili and milk and ice cream sourced from four different companies, a hassle embraced because no one company meets their needs and quality demands.

The Sea Swirl's glass-and-chrome build-ing speaks to its roots as a Carvel ice cream stand.

Architecture buffs drool over the Sea Swirl's glass-and-chrome googie retro building; beach lovers get sea smells and some nice sunsets from tented picnic tables overlooking a tidal marsh. (There is no indoor seating.)

The result has been coverage and accolades from Rachel Ray and the *New York Times* on down to the local *New London Day* (which called them "the best of the best" Connecticut clam shacks).

The Sea Swirl opened as a Carvel ice cream stand in 1950, but it was mid-1980s purchasers Kathleen and Dave Blaney who set its current high

Plumber-restaurateur Ryan Devlin-Perry

standards. "We like fried clams, but we don't like them dark and greasy. When we eat fish, we don't want a frozen stick. We put ourselves in the footsteps of our customers," Dave recalled on the 25th anniversary of his ownership. A year later, the Blaneys sold the Sea Swirl to a longtime customer concerned about the future availability of his beloved Sea Swirl hot dogs and black-and-white shakes.

Mark Adams delegated the day-to-day running of the stand to son-in-law Ryan Devlin-Perry, a plumber who brings a tradesman's practicality to his summer gig. Asked about the Swirl's proudest achievements, he replies, "That we run like a machine," rather than with the expected list of best dishes. For him, the Sea Swirl is an operation, and consistency and efficiency the goals.

The golf-ball-sized, Drum Rock-based clam fritters are a holdover from the Blaneys' reign and are among the stand's top five sellers (fried clams with bellies, codfish sandwiches, fish and chips, and lobster rolls are the others). His aim with the fritters is that there be "clams in every one and that they're not too dense.

"Good but not perfect," he says while trying one with a visitor *who he knows is going to write about them*. Amazing!

"With more water, they'd be less dense. But if you put too much, the batter splatters and you get a lot of protrusions," he mused aloud with a serious expression.

Early in the second summer of COVID, he bemoaned the cost of cooking oil and clams, as well as finding high school employees who know their six times tables (so they can drop the proper amount of fritter batter for multiple half-dozen orders).

Pandemic-era challenges notwithstanding, many other seafood stand owners spoke of the joys of being the source of summertime treats like clam cakes and ice cream.

But you get the feeling Devlin-Perry would be happier alone in a bathroom clearing a clogged drain.

>> If the line is too long at Sea Swirl, you might want to drive three minutes down Route 27 to the **Sea View** (145 Greenmanville Ave., Mystic, CT, 860-572-0096). Although the Swirl might have more food cred, the Sea View lives up to its name with a much superior setting on the banks of the Mystic River. Sea View operator Michelle Wood Mansee has goosed this naturally great location with hanging flower baskets and manicured hedges. There is also a rough-hewn charm about the aquamarine wooden takeout stand and picnic pavilion built with too-long nails. (Look up while getting your condiments if you don't believe me.) As for the clam fritters: They're dark, nubbin-less, and quite salty.

SUMMER SHACK
1 MOHEGAN SUN BLVD., MONTVILLE, CT, 860-862-9500,
SUMMERSHACKRESTAURANT.COM

Mohegan Sun is the only place in New England where you can gamble only steps away from a consoling big plate of clam fritters. You can get them at either of two Summer Shacks in that casino: the full-service restaurant or its express takeout offshoot. Both are as much like real New England clam shacks as Las Vegas's New York New York resort is like the real NYC—which is to say, not very. But it's still fun and worth visiting.

The first Summer Shack chef Jasper White opened in Cambridge, Massachusetts, in 2000 took Boston by storm and surprise. What was the chef behind renowned fine-dining destination Jasper's doing opening an everyman fish hall?

Giving his fans more of the seafood they wanted. In its first two years, Jasper's went from 50/50 seafood/meat to an almost-all-seafood menu because of how people were ordering. Summer Shack was also White trying to re-create—and slightly elevate—the food and kick-back atmosphere he enjoyed at seafood joints near family summer places in Little Compton, Rhode Island, and coastal Maine, he explains in the introduction to his *Summer Shack Cookbook*.

The early days of that first Summer Shack were barely controlled chaos, with soccer moms running from the parking lot to snag one of the big picnic tables, kids running around checking out the big lobster pots and raw shellfish displays, and waiters running around with big platters of fried everything.

This similar Summer Shack opened at Mohegan Sun one year later, though the darkness of the windowless building makes it hard to see the decorations and equipment and the din of the gambling machines dampens the boisterousness of groups dining at the big picnic tables. (The much fewer kids in the casino setting also contributes to the different feel.)

White sold all his Summer Shacks in 2017, but the Mohegan Sun one still makes White's original signature pan-roasted lobster, fried chicken, and clam fritters.

The fritters are dark, crusty, and full of non-clam flavors—they actually seem more like Southern hush puppies than Rhode Island clam cakes. I chalked this up to the cornmeal and scallions in White's recipe, which manager Tricia Distefano says they still use, though, in a separate interview, chef Jefferson Magalhaes admitted to also adding garlic, shallot, and even some Cajun seasoning.

But what Summer Shack clam fritters lack in authenticity they make up for in high standards of preparation and ingredients. Theirs is among the few to feature quahogs, which are more flavorful and expensive than the sea clams more often used. And they come with house-made tartar.

In fact, in the monument to chance and uncertainty that is Mohegan Sun, these clam fritters are as close as you're going to get to a sure good thing.

A New England Seafood God on Clam Fritters

Jasper White once described an idyllic afternoon as "an oceanside bar or restaurant, draft beer, steamers, a few friends" and "a few side orders of"—not lobster, not fried clams—but "clam fritters."

So it's no wonder that fritters were on the menu when White launched his Summer Shack restaurant concept in 2000, and have been a thing at its Connecticut iteration for more than 20 years since.

There's also a practical explanation. "A lot of people can't afford fried clams," White says on the phone from his home on the Massachusetts coast. "Fritters are a great alternative: They can feed a lot of people with only a handful of clams."

This leading authority on New England seafood cookery actually grew up near the New Jersey Shore. But White's ex-wife was from Rhode Island, and he says his idea of clam cakes is rooted in visits to Evelyn's in Tiverton with her.

But Evelyn's clam cakes contain neither scallions nor cornmeal.

"I'm a James Beard-award-winning chef. I wasn't just going to just flatly copy," he responds, a tiny bit testily.

He also didn't just make fritters with clams: corn and oyster, corn and crab, and apple have all had their moments in Summer Shack's fritter spotlight.

Beaches Near the Fritters in Connecticut

Most of Connecticut's shoreline beaches are on Long Island Sound and, therefore, relatively calm. Fees are parking for nonresidents in the summer. (Some beaches offer discounted rates starting in the late afternoon.)

Hammonasset Beach State Park, 1288 Boston Post Rd., Madison. Connecticut's largest public beach, with a popular campground. $15/$22 weekdays/weekends.

Ocean Beach Park, 98 Neptune Ave., New London. The beach is only the beginning: This place also has an Olympic-sized swimming pool, a boardwalk, miniature golf, an arcade, a nature trail, a picnic area, and, in the summer, a whole lot of people. $25/$30 weekdays/weekends.

Williams Beach Park, 1 Harry Austin Dr., Mystic. Public beach on the Mystic River with a playground and free parking and access courtesy of the Mystic YMCA.

Now that White is retired, he makes clam fritters from clams he harvests himself. "I found this really good spot on Cape Cod for cherrystones, razor clams—you never really know what you're going to find."

White was happy to share his clam fritters recipe (which follows) and fritter-making tips (see pp. 154–155). But ask for the location of this great clamming spot and he clams up.

Jasper White's Clam Fritters

4 to 5 pounds small quahogs or large cherrystone clams, shells rinsed and scrubbed clean

2 cups all-purpose flour

2 teaspoons baking powder

4 eggs, lightly beaten

4 tablespoons unsalted butter

1 cup milk

1 cup jonnycake meal or cornmeal

½ cup minced scallions

½ teaspoon salt

1 teaspoon black pepper

Peanut, corn, canola, or other vegetable oil for frying

Pour ½ cup water in a large pot, cover, and bring to a boil over medium-high heat. Add clams, re-cover, and steam until the clams have opened, about 10 to 15 minutes. Cool, shuck, and chop the clams, reserving and straining 1 cup of their broth from the shells and the pot.

In a large bowl, combine the flour, baking powder, and eggs and mix well. Place the butter, milk, and clam juice in a small saucepan and heat just until it starts to simmer and the butter is melted. Stir in the cornmeal and let sit for 5 to 10 minutes. Then add the cornmeal mixture to the flour/egg one. Fold in the chopped clams, scallions, and salt and pepper. Batter should be somewhat thick. Cover and refrigerate for at least an hour.

Heat fryolator to 375°F. Drop the batter into the oil by the tablespoonful and fry until golden brown, about 3 to 4 minutes, turning frequently so the fritters brown evenly. Drain on paper towels and serve hot.

Yield: 24 1½-inch fritters

MASSACHUSETTS

CAPTAIN FROSTY'S
219 MAIN ST., DENNIS, MA, 508-385-8548, CAPTAINFROSTY.COM

There are almost as many clam shacks on Cape Cod roadsides as rose hips and orange daylilies. Few have clam cakes. Captain Frosty's to the rescue with a lifesaving menu that includes two clam cakes on every dinner plate, clam cake appetizers by the half-dozen, dozen, and two dozen, and cakes as part of a combination meal with chowder and coleslaw.

Captain Frosty's classy interior

Captain Frosty's name and glassy sloped-roof building reveal its mid-1950s roots as a soft-serve ice cream stand. A less sophisticated owner would be blasting 1950s music and hosting classic car nights there now.

Instead, 1976 purchasers Mike and Patricia Henderson added two park-like patios and a lodge-like knotty pine indoor dining room decorated with bait bucket planters, framed vintage Cape Cod postcards—even a wire basket of classic sea-themed reads. Although unusual for a clam shack, Captain Frosty's classiness fits its Route 6-A neighborhood of historic homes and antiques stores.

The Hendersons were also behind the menu expansion to seafood, including the clam cakes Pat knew and loved from growing up in Rhode Island. "But practically nobody on the Cape was familiar with them," she explained recently. Hence the idea of including two free clam cakes with every seafood platter by way of education.

It's a tradition her son, current owner Matt Henderson, continues, though at this point, he sees the clam cakes more as "a way of filling out the plate," like hush puppies do in the South. And like hush puppies, "Clam cakes are easy to like," especially when they come "free" with the meal.

Frosty's has also made numerous best-of lists for their fried clams, lobster rolls, and fish and chips. The latter are breaded, rather than battered, and made with cod rather than the more usual haddock. Matt likes cod's meatiness.

All seafood is sourced locally (except for the not-local shrimp and salmon), although Henderson laments that this is becoming more difficult every year. "Every year distributors come in here trying to sell me pre-frozen this or vacuum-packed that, trying to break down that castle wall. I've really resisted that and will continue to . . . until fresh stuff just isn't available anymore," he finishes wearily.

Captain Frosty's also still does a brisk soft-serve ice cream business. In fact, the outdoor ordering window on Route 6-A is only for ice cream, and Henderson thinks some people who order there "aren't even aware we have food." Frozen favorites include the orange freeze (like a liquid Creamsicle) and Yoberry frozen yogurt, whose devotees show up for on closing weekend to stock up for the long Yoberryless winter.

All offerings are spelled out on the original 1950s illuminated menu boards, changes to which must be hand-painted—thus increasing the likelihood that the Captain Frosty's food you love today will still be there the next time you visit. And on the visit after that.

EGG ROLL LADY AND FISH SHACK
609 W. BOYLSTON ST., WORCESTER, MA, 508-755-4451

"Hush puppies with pieces of clam" is a common—though not entirely accurate—way to describe RI-style clam fritters to a Southerner. (Clam fritters are traditionally lots doughier.) But it's an apt description for the clam fritters sold at the Egg Roll Lady and Fish Shack.

They're crispy all the way through and flavored with scallion and sweet pepper, as well as clam. In other words, they're as different from the standard Southern New England issue cakes as the Egg Roll Lady—aka Phuong Lam—is from the typical clam shack owner.

Lam was one of about 800,000 "boat people" who escaped Vietnam's oppressive Communist regime between 1975 and 1995. When the Communists took over, Lam says dozens of husbands and fathers in her town were summoned to a day of "re-education" from which they never returned.

Phuong Lam, aka the Egg Roll Lady, in front of her fish "shack"

Her 1987 ocean escape from Vietnam to Malaysia in a boat "weaker than a canoe" took four days. Lam spent nine months in a refugee camp in the

Philippines before arriving in the United States; at first, in Portland, Oregon (where she met her future husband), before moving to Worcester, Massachusetts, on the promise of a job.

When not working at that medical equipment gig, Lam cooked up gifts of food—including flaky Vietnamese egg rolls filled with pork, chicken, cabbage, carrot, and garlic—for co-workers, fellow church members, aid workers, and basically anyone who had helped her or whom she thought needed help.

"I can express myself cooking better than with words," she explains.

By 1999, this practice morphed into an idea to start a weekend fair concession side hustle. "This was tough for me because I don't know anything about this and I had to buy a trailer, even though I had no money." And most of the fairs were hours from her home.

"I would get home from the fair at 3 a.m. then have to be back at 11. I was always late. . . . Customers who were looking for me would go to the office and say, 'Where is the Egg Roll Lady?'"

That's how she got her name, which Lam loves, by the way. "It's so cute."

After seven years of juggling the fairs with a full-time job and raising three girls with husband Bao Bui, "I start to feel tired. I go online looking for a little store."

What she found was a tiny former fish and chip shop with only four tables encased in iron security grating on a busy street just off I-90.

At first the plan was to just replicate her fair menu of egg rolls, barbecue pork, and chicken with rice. But then she thought: Why not take advantage of the business the Fish Shack had built up?

Hence the Egg Roll Lady and Fish Shack's unusual amalgam of delicious fried foods from East and West.

Lam inherited the clam fritter recipe from the Fish Shack but thought it too plain. So she scoured cookbooks and YouTube before coming up with her crusty balls flavored with scallion and green and red bell pepper (to mitigate saltiness) and the same chopped clams she uses in her clam chowder. "If you dip in chowder, it's so good," she says.

Nevertheless, Lam was initially wary of being featured in a clam fritter book. "I'm not strong with the fritters the way I am with egg roll," she claimed, her Phantom Gourmet YouTube-famous smile turned upside down.

And it's true that she is the Egg Roll Lady and not the Clam Fritter Lady.

At least until now.

Savory Doughnut Holes: A World Tour

There are only so many good ways to prepare and cook food—hence the parallel dishes across cultures. Almost every cuisine has some kind of pancake and dumpling, for instance. And as weird as the Rhode Island-style clam cakes might seem, they are not the world's only savory doughnut holes.

Among the others:

Hush puppies. The standard comparison for US clam cake first-timers, probably because hush puppies are so popular all over the South. But hush puppies are usually a side dish, have no protein focal point, and are crispy all the way through, instead of just on the outside, because of being made with cornmeal, instead of flour, as with a proper Rhode Island clam cake.

Conch fritters. The national dish of the Bahamas and very similar to clam cakes, these can also be found on other Caribbean Islands and South Florida, especially the Keys. As with the clams used in clam cakes, conch (snail) can be tough, so they are finely cut up. Conch's flavor is mild compared to clam, so conch fritters are usually amped up with chopped onions, celery, and bell peppers. Like clam cakes, they're often served with chowder (in this case, the conch kind).

Buñuelos de bacalao. Popular Spanish tapas, quite similar to clam cakes, except for featuring salt cod instead of clams and potato in addition to flour. Salt cod fritters are also a thing in Portugal, where they are called *pasteis de bacalhau*, and in Italy, where they are known as *baccala* or *frittelle di baccala*. *Baccala* also show up at a lot of Italian-American Christmas Eve Feasts of the Seven Fishes.

Pakoras. Indian street snack made by mixing grated vegetables like potato and cauliflower into a thin batter made of chickpea flour, water, and Indian spices. The resulting shape, when the batter hits hot oil, is all over the place, like an all-nubbin clam cake.

Takoyaki. Extremely popular Japanese street food and convenience store snack featuring octopus. In addition to clam cakes' flour, egg, and leavening, these usually contain soy sauce, pickled ginger, and dashi. They're also usually pan- rather than deep-fried, have a gooey versus a doughy interior, and are adorned with various sauces. But like clam cakes, they are ball-shaped snacks showcasing a sometimes-maligned seafood.

KATE'S SEAFOOD
284 PAINES CREEK RD., BREWSTER, MA, 508-896-9517,
LIAMSANDKATES.COM

Most of the restaurants in this book are on their second or third owners. And not that many people put their names on their own businesses anymore.

But when you go to Kate's Seafood in Brewster, Massachusetts, there's a good chance of being waited on by THE Kate Ohman or, what is perhaps even more exciting for onion ring fans, her son, Liam.

Liam is the namesake of a former also-Ohman-owned seafood shack that was famous for their

Liam and Kate Ohman, with their Drum Rock clam fritters

onion rings. In the most important ways (of food and personnel), Kate's is Kate's plus Liam's stand reincarnated.

Kate's came first. Kate's husband and Liam's father, John Ohman, was a longtime operator of beach concessions and food trucks when he bought this little red-and-white building in 1986. He didn't take over the former Philbrick's Nauset Beach concession—renaming it after his newborn son—until 1990.

But the popularity of that beach and the fried onion ring recipe that Ohman inherited from Philbrick's made Liam's famous.

Ohman lost the lease on Liam's at Nauset after a 2017 coastal storm led town leaders to rethink the parking lot and concession setup. It's a decision that the grown-up Liam describes while still-visibly upset. (Understandably—his name *was* on the building, after all.) But it lives on in him and several other former Liam's employees who now make and serve the onion rings and other seafood specialties at Kate's.

Yankee magazine once described these onion rings as not "onions, or rings, or food" but "sacraments." Sister Agnes would call that blasphemy—I'd say it's a stretch. But they are hand-cut, very sweet, and covered with a delicious, thin, tempura-style crust that Kate's now also uses to fry up zucchini, mushroom, and pepper rings (or a combo plate of all three).

As for the reason we're even talking about Kate's: Her clam fritters are competently executed Drum Rock containing more than the usual amount of sea clams and served gratis two to every dinner plate like they are at the nearby Captain Frosty's—and almost nowhere else in Southern New England.

Did Kate's crib clam fritters from that older place? Kate rejects this theory, saying the idea to put them on the menu came from her husband and employee clam fritter fans.

What else to get while you're there? Kate calls her scallops "amazing." And the New England-style cold lobster rolls, lightly dressed with mayonnaise, have many Yelp fans.

This is not to mention Kate's 51 flavors of ice cream, five flavors of frozen yogurt, and two sorbets (from Gifford's and Hood).

Although Kate's has two picnic areas to eat these treats, a lot of people buy Kate's food or ice cream to go eat at Paine's Creek Beach, just half a mile down the road. In fact, one local man with a tractor named Sparky has made a 30-year-old symbiotic business of giving Kate's customers a hayride to and from that beach's famed sunsets.

How Famous Were/Are Liam's Onion Rings?

So famous that one day a man came into the stand asking for an order of the smallest possible onion rings. He picked one out of the carton, then went out to the beach and proposed to his boyfriend.

After that, it became a Liam's tradition to send orders of onion rings out to any wedding taking place on Nauset Beach.

TONY'S CLAM SHOP
861 QUINCY SHORE DR., QUINCY, MA, 617-773-5090,
TONYSCLAMSHOP.COM

"We use Drum Rock but we add our own spices," Tony's Clam Shop manager Shawn Bulman proclaimed, echoing the words of dozens of other professional clam fritter makers who use that prepared fritter mix, and my heart sank. Spices in New England usually mean salt and pepper, and I braced myself for a standard-issue fritter.

Tony's fried fish trust includes (left to right) chef Hakim Gherbi, owner Gary Kandalaft, and manager Shawn Bulman.

Imagine my surprise, then, when I bit into one of Tony's maple-brown fried golf balls to see caution-sign-yellow dough and taste spices that kicked my mind out of New England and into the Middle East. This is clam fritter meets falafel, which makes perfect sense considering that Tony's was founded by Lebanese-Syrian-American Tony Kandalaft and is now owned and run by his grown-up kids.

When the Kandalafts bought into this working-class beach neighborhood in 1964, the building was a combination house/walk-up window clam shack. A one-way mirror in the living room let them know when a customer arrived. As the business grew, grills and refrigerators filled the bedrooms, and the family had to find somewhere else to live.

Today, Tony's is a sprawling space across a busy street from Wollaston Beach with multiple seating options, including a back garden, a greenhouse-like indoor dining room, and an open-air patio. Although a fair number of people take out to the sea wall across the street for a more direct view of the Boston skyline and, on one recent late Sunday morning, the tiny white triangles of a distant sailing class.

Tony's is known for the usual fried clams, fish and chips, and salad-style lobster rolls (though the hot-butter variety is gaining fans) as well as the less-usual deep-fried battered lobster, fountain-made raspberry lime rickeys (made locally popular by the old Brigham's ice cream chain), chicken kebobs, and the clam fritters. The kebobs are one of two items left from what used to be a whole Middle Eastern section of the menu—one of three, if you count the spicy fritters.

Bulman says the first clam cakes sold at Tony's were Maine-style patties purchased frozen. They switched to the Rhode Island balls due to (presumably Rhode Island) customer complaints. Reasons Bulman, "The fritter style goes better with chowder, anyway." That chowder is white and homemade: The structural integrity of its potatoes lends proof to Bulman's claim.

Tony's chef, Hakim Gherbi, adds clam juice and sea clams to Drum Rock mix to make their clam fritters, but Jubilee brand seafood seasoning is the key to their unique interior hue and spicy taste. Unique to out-of-towners, anyway: This seems to be the standard profile for fritters on Wollaston Beach. (See side story on Tony's competitor, The Clam Box.) Wollaston is also one of few places you'll see ball-style clam fritters serve as the focal point of a dinner platter with French fries.

Some Rhode Island clam cake traditionalists deem Tony's clam fritters a little too out there, but Bulman and Gherbi don't care. Says Bulman: "The clam cakes in Rhode Island are very boring."

>> If the lines are too long at Tony's, walk five minutes up the street to **The Clam Box** (789 Quincy Shore Dr., Wollaston Beach, MA, 617-773-6677, clamboxquincy.com), the only other restaurant in the world making clam cakes for people who'd rather be eating kofta kebobs. If anything, The Clam Box's clam cakes are even more aggressively spiced than Tony's. They're also darker and bigger: baseball- versus golf-ball-sized. The rest of the menu and the building are very similar to Tony's, though this place is older and, fast-food history-wise, more important: Forty-three years before opening as The Clam Box in 1968, this was the world's second Howard Johnson's.

WOODMAN'S OF ESSEX
119 MAIN ST., ESSEX, MA, 978-768-6451, WOODMANS.COM

Most people go to Woodman's for its reputed role as the birthplace of the fried clam or because they deem it the best of the four clam stands that make up Route 133 Massachusetts's celebrated "Clam Highway."

Woodman's giant clam sign

We favor it as the only one of these famed fried clam shacks to also make clam cakes.

In fact, the fried clam origin story in the restaurant's official history suggests that one reason clam and potato chip vendors Chubby and Bessie Woodman found a friend's suggestion to cook up clams in their potato chip fryer worth a try (in 1916, in this very place!) was Bessie's habit of frying up clam cakes at home.

The story serves as a reminder that clam cakes likely came first, and certainly were made and enjoyed long before Howard Johnson's made fried clams famous.

Nowadays, Woodman's renown nearly rivals Howard Johnson's. The stand has racked up countless media mentions and awards, including Best Waterside Seafood Shack in the USA (*USA Today*), Best Seafood in America (*Forbes FYI*), and Best Place to Eat in the state (*Bon Appetit*). It is also, perhaps not coincidentally, the only seafood shack in this book with an online pressroom.

Woodman's actual physical reality is, by contrast, surprisingly rough-hewn. With its rows of worn wooden booths, the dining room resembles an old saloon or somebody's back porch. (Aunt Carrie's dining room is also more than a century old and plain but shows evidence of having gotten fresh coats of paint and varnish sometime recently.)

That's why in nice weather it's probably better to get your fill of the historic atmosphere while ordering and eat at one of the picnic tables beside the peaceful salt marsh out back. At least it's peaceful during the off-season and during the day. The combination of free live music and Woodman's bar reportedly makes this more of a fun party place on summer evenings.

Although Woodman's may be famous for fried clams, on summer weekends, lobster is what's front and center on the sidewalk in front of the building. Step up to the ordering window inside and you'll see a helpful display of all the different-sized cups and containers used for the food but only one actual food sample—of the clam cakes. That's for the many Bay Staters who've never heard of them and for the few who know the Maine kind and think that's what Woodman's is making.

Woodman's co-CEO Stephen Woodman ate a Maine-style clam cake once but has never had a Rhode Island-style one other than his own. Unencumbered by Drum Rock or Aunt Carrie's standards, Woodman is simply trying to faithfully execute his grandmother Bessie's recipe—a recipe that is, by the way, published in *Woodman's of Essex: Five Generations of Stories and 100 Years of Recipes* and also here, with his permission. The idea that other restaurateurs might copy it has either not occurred to him or he could care less. In any case, it's refreshing.

Woodman is similarly open when answering questions about how Woodman's makes their clam cakes: It's with lard and chopped sea clams from Nantucket Shoals, he says without hesitation (though Woodman's fried clams are made with Essex-area soft-shells).

He also admits to tweaking Bessie's clam cake recipe in two ways: 1. They now use a clam juice reduction in place of the called-for water because "it's more flavorful." 2. They're now golf-ball- rather than squash-ball-sized, not to save money—"because actually, now, we give people more"—but to up the crustiness.

The result is a hearty (though not heavy) cake with a wonderful crunch and appendages that reminded me of some other clam dish I'd had before—wait, it's fried clams! So these are like clam cakes with little pieces of fried clam stuck to the sides or like two fried clam dishes in one. At $2.50 for two (or actually three smaller-sized cakes), they are the cheapest food on Woodman's menu and one of this book's biggest bargains.

In recent years, Woodman's has tried to boost their revenues and visibility by inviting in movie production companies. Their scenes in *Mermaids* and *Grown Ups* have yet to produce the kind of "I'll have what she's having" moment that brought fame to New York's Katz's Deli, or much buzz at all, actually.

They don't need it. So long as they keep making those fried clams and clam cakes.

Spoiler Alert

One two-inch Rhode Island-style clam cake contains about 150 calories, 5 grams of fat, and 400 grams of sodium. If only you could order just one. Traditionally, the only options are a half-dozen or dozen. That's 1,800 calories and 60 grams of fat or approaching fisherman's platter territory, if you eat all 12 of them yourself.

One three-ounce deep-fried Maine-style clam cake contains about 150 calories, 7 grams of fat, and 730 milligrams of sodium. Putting it on a hamburger bun doubles the calories.

This leaves the Virginia-style pan-fried clam fritter the clear nutritional winner at about 120 calories, 2 grams of fat, and 120 milligrams of sodium. Although that is without a bun or the sides that almost everyone eats them with.

Nana Bessie Woodman's Clam Cakes

1 cup all-purpose flour

2 teaspoons baking powder

¼ teaspoon salt

1 egg

1 cup minced clams (juice strained and reserved)

3 tablespoons of reserved clam juice (or clam juice plus water, if you don't have enough juice)

Lard (or Crisco), for frying

In a medium mixing bowl, combine flour, baking powder, and salt. Add egg, clams, and clam juice and mix until well-blended, about 2 or 3 minutes. A mixer with a dough hook works best; if you don't have one, use a spoon. The mixture will be sticky, but you should be able to roll it into a ball with your fingers. If the mixture is too sticky to form a ball, add more flour until you can.

In a fryolator or frying pan with tall sides, add enough lard to melt to at least 1 or 1½ inches of oil. Then heat oil to 325°F. Using a teaspoon, make small, round balls, and gently put them into the fat and cook 3 to 5 minutes or until golden brown and cooked throughout.

Yield: 2 servings

Beaches Near the Fritters/Cakes in Massachusetts

Fees are parking for nonresidents in the summer.

Quincy

Wollaston Beach, Quincy Shore Dr., Quincy. Rocky beach on Boston Harbor occasionally closed for run-off. On the upside: Free, on-street parking.

Near Dennis/Brewster on Cape Cod

On the Cape, beaches are either bay- or oceanside, the former being a lot calmer than the latter.

Corporation, Corporation Rd., Dennis. Bayside beach with a snack bar. $30.

Mayflower Beach, 2 Dunes View Rd., Dennis. Go at low tide and explore the tide pools. $20/$25 weekdays/weekends.

Nauset Beach, 250 Beach Rd., Orleans. Ten-mile-long ocean beach favored for big waves and long walks. $30.

Paine's Creek Beach, 143 Cedar Hill Rd., Brewster. Another bay-side beach great for low-tide exploring. Limited parking for $20.

Sandy Neck Beach, 425 Sandy Neck Rd., West Barnstable. Bay-side stony beach popular with RVs. $15.

West Dennis Beach, West Dennis Beach Rd., West Dennis. Sound-side beach with volleyball, shelling, and windsurfing. $30.

Near Essex

Crane Beach, 310 Argilla Rd., Ipswich. Known for its seaside forest and role as a nesting site for Piping Plovers. Big with Beantowners looking to escape the city quickly. $40/$45 weekdays/weekends.

Wingaersheek Beach, 298 Atlantic St., Gloucester. Great family beach with tide pools ripe for exploring. $30/$35 weekday/weekend (pre-registration required).

Clam Cake Part-Timers

With so many places profiled in this book making clam cakes every day, some even year-round, it might seem reasonable to dismiss any-place that only makes them once or twice a week.

Reasonable but a mistake.

Though the author of a book called *The Great Clam Cake and Fritter Guide* may be prejudiced, I say the more clam cakes, the better.

If you're wondering after looking at the following list why so many places make their clam cakes on Friday: It's customer habit born of the days when Southern New England's many Roman Catho-lics were prohibited from eating meat on Fridays.

Buttonwoods Fish & Chips, 416 Buttonwoods Ave., Warwick, RI, 401-738-7571, buttonwoods416.com. Home-style restaurant known for their breakfasts, hot wieners, and fish and chips. Their clam cakes, made with Drum Rock mix, are served Thursdays and Fridays.

Don's Diner, 121 South St., Plainville, MA, 508-695-7036, dons dinerrestaurant.com. This near-pristine 1952 Mountain View diner dishes up their own clam cakes on Friday nights (and for Saturday lunch, if there's batter left). They're spongy inside and crunchy out and contain minced quahog. Order them with a side of also-so-New England baked beans and a Natalie Burger, a hamburger/grilled cheese hybrid named for its policewoman/Don's regular inventor.

Johnny's Clam Shack, 184 North Main St., Norwich, CT, 860-710-7361, johnnysclamshack.com. John Oliveira makes clam cakes using Drum Rock mix on Mondays at his titular seasonal clam shack for the Rocky Point-nostalgic but admits to mixed feelings about it. "They're a lot of work for not a lot of money, and they really decimate my fryer capacity. This is a really small restaurant." There's also the problem of people who come for them on the wrong day and "get very annoyed."

Stadium Fish & Chips, 1079 Park Ave., Cranston, RI, 401-944-0971. Storied fish and chippery dating back to the early 1940s. Makes clam cakes with Kenyon's mix on Thursdays.

Stanley's Famous Hamburgers, 535 Dexter St., Central Falls, RI, 401-726-9689, stanleyshamburgers.com. Go on Fridays to get a side of Drum Rock clam cakes with their signature Stanley burger, made with fresh-ground beef, grilled onions, and pickles since the early 1930s.

Willow Tree, 997 South Main St., Attleboro, MA, 508-222-2479, willowtreefarm.com. Willow Tree's chicken salad is discussed on p. 37. This former poultry farm is probably even more famous for its chicken pies. Both are sold in supermarkets and delis throughout New England, as well as at this company store, where they make Drum Rock-based clam cakes on Wednesdays in the summer.

MAINE-STYLE CLAM CAKES

Those in search of great Maine clam cakes should maintain a laser-like focus on the clam shacks on one spot on the state's 3,500-mile coast: the Saco-Scarborough area just south of Portland.

Going to be somewhere else in Maine? All is not lost, thanks to Harmon's, a company with World War II-era Scarborough restaurant roots whose clam cakes are cooked up with pride by seafood shacks up and down the Maine coast.

HUOT'S SEAFOOD RESTAURANT
29 EASTERN AVE., SACO, ME, 207-282-1642, HUOTSSEAFOOD.COM

Huot's sold a record 3,800 clam cakes the last day they were open for the 2021 season.

The last day is normally always big, with locals returning for a last meal or to stock up on frozen clam cakes to get them through a long Maine winter.

But with the news that Huot's was up for sale, some people were stocking up for their lifetimes.

Fear not, people. A seasonal restaurant that gets lines on a mid-afternoon weekday in September is not just going to go away. And in fact, Huot's was purchased by a group of former customers a few months later. The main cause of that purchase and those lines: Huot's famous clam cakes.

"Harmon's are pasty and powdery and have more clam juice than clams. These are real tasty and flavorful," says Jim Douglas of Westbrook, Maine, there to surprise his wife with some clam cake takeout.

Out back in the graveled picnic area, friends Deb Buxton and Judy Ware took their plastic forks and knives to a late lunch of two clam cakes each. Clam cakes and nothing else.

Asked how Huot's clam cakes compare with others in the area, Buxton replies, "They don't compare. These are handmade with a crispy batter and lots of pieces of clam and are good-sized.

"Usually I only get one," she continues, apologetically. "But Huot's is closing next week so we're splurging."

Huot's clam cakes are indeed larger and thicker than most other Maine-style ones, with a soufflé-like middle and a batter crust to rival the best Austrian schnitzel.

Denise Huot Gelinas with Huot's most-beloved dish

In fact, in three visits to Huot's, the only mixed thing uttered about their clam cakes was from then-owner Denise Huot Gelinas herself.

"Ours are bigger than a lot of other places. We're also known to have a lot of clams. Some people prefer Ken's or The Clambake or Harmon's, because that's what they're used to," said Gelinas from a booth on a break from prep work.

Huot's is the definition of family restaurant in more than one way. The dining room of this simple, squat building located only about 450 feet from the water is filled with families and senior citizens sitting at the same booths and reading (almost) the same menu by the same lobster-adorned lamps as when Gelinas's grandparents started pressing clams and cracker pieces into patties here in 1935.

Gelinas began working at Huot's when she was 10 and got her husband, Gerry, a job at Huot's when they were high school sweethearts.

Denise earned her teaching degree but "felt obligated" to help out when her father got older, although she says the seasonal business "worked out" for raising her kids. Despite working at Huot's each summer starting at age 14 (or perhaps because of it), the Gelinas's two daughters apparently felt no such sense of obligation about continuing the family business. Hence, the sale.

How did longtime customers take the news?

Actually, Gelinas says, not as badly as when Huot's eliminated waitress service. Although they did this as a cost-cutting measure in 2018, it helped during the pandemic. "I know a lot of businesses had to close even after the restrictions were lifted because they didn't have enough help."

Her response to complaints about this and their pandemic suspension of phone orders:

"We're not doing brain surgery here. You're going to get your food, and we're all going to survive," she says, noting the usefulness of her college minor in psychology.

All-takeout also meant no more boiled lobster and surf and turf dinners because "they don't travel well." And additional outrage ensued.

All of which led Gelinas to advise restaurant vet/new Huot's managing partner Alan Waugh and friends to keep to the course her family has charted. It's advice they've taken to heart, judging by the introductory Facebook post pledging to follow Huot family recipes, including Gelinas's grandmother Doris's clam cake one.

Gelinas says she was very young when Doris Huot died and remembers her mostly from the restaurant. "She worked a lot of hours. I think she liked it, but I remember when she got cancer, they put a chair out where she used to sit down sometimes. She worked until the very end. There was really no one there to run it for her."

Who could blame Gelinas for possibly trying to duck a similar fate?

French-Canadian Salmon Pie

Another Huot's specialty possibly even more prized than their clam cakes is salmon pie. That's partly because this is pie covered with gravy or comfort food to-the-max and partly because of its limited availability: Even during the Huots' reign, salmon pie was only sold on Fridays because, Denise Gelinas says, "It's very time-consuming to make."

In fact, salmon pie and its meat pie counterpart are typically winter-holiday-only fare for New England French-Canadian families like the Huots. The restaurant's new owners have yet to bring it back. Here's a recipe (not Huot's) to tide you over until they do.

Pie

3 cups mashed potatoes (from about 2 pounds potato)

1 medium onion, finely chopped

2 tablespoons butter

¼ cup milk, 2 tablespoons reserved

½ teaspoon celery salt

½ teaspoon garlic salt

½ teaspoon salt

14 to 15 ounces of salmon, either canned or cooked from fresh, minus bones, skin, and liquid

2 tablespoons fresh parsley, minced

2 (9-inch) pie crusts, top and bottom, store-bought or homemade

Sauce

- 3 tablespoons butter
- 3 tablespoons all-purpose flour
- 1 cup milk
- 2 tablespoons lemon juice
- 1 tablespoon fresh dill, chopped
- Salt and pepper to taste

For the pie: Preheat oven to 350°F. In a large bowl, combine the mashed potatoes, onion, butter, all but 2 tablespoons of the milk, and the three salts. Flake the salmon with a fork then blend into the potato mixture along with the parsley.

Line a 9-inch pie plate with one crust and trim the edges. Fill the shell with the salmon mixture. Cover with top crust and seal and flute edges. Vent the top crust with slits, then brush it with the remaining milk. Cook for 25 to 35 minutes or until crust is golden brown.

For the sauce: Melt the butter in a small saucepan over medium heat. Add the flour and whisk until smooth. Gradually add the milk while stirring constantly. When the sauce begins to thicken, add the lemon juice, dill, and salt and pepper to taste. Keep warm until ready to serve. Drizzle over pie.

Yield: 8 servings

KEN'S PLACE
207 PINE POINT RD., SCARBOROUGH, ME, 207-883-6611

Ken's is one of two restaurants that come up most frequently in any search for the best Maine clam cakes. (See Huot's on p. 102 for the other.)

Clam cakes were the first and only menu item when clam digger Ken Skilling opened this place in 1927, and it's still their most famous dish. On a busy day, they'll sell 600.

The original Ken's building was Skilling's garage. The second, a tiny stand now used for storage, is dwarfed by the current big, gray elephant of a takeout stand he built in 1950. A second owner, the Bergerons, enclosed the open-air porches, giving today's diners

their pick of three dining rooms and outdoor picnic tables under pines. Restrooms are in a separate building in back and signed like they were the main attraction. Ditto for the sign screaming SEAFOODS (and grammatical error) from both sides of the main building. Glamorous and modern this is not.

Ken's is, instead, a classic roadside destination and age-old tradition for generations of local families. Despite the restaurant's seasonal schedule and location between the popular Pine Point and Old Orchard beaches, 60 to 70 percent of customers are local. Ken's biggest sales day isn't even in the summer! It's Mother's Day. (Father's Day is next.)

Sales have quadrupled since Dave Wilcox bought Ken's in 2000. "Consistency, quality, and excellent staff" is how Wilcox explains it. Other obvious factors: This thin, wiry, and seriously focused man's hard work and respect for tradition. Ken's Place still batters and breads their own fish and makes their own clam and fish chowders and clam cakes daily.

"Ken's wife used to form the cakes by hand, like you would hamburger," Wilcox says, while patting the batter into metal rings on a tray that he uses. And Wilcox stores his cracker meal in a big bin made of plastic, instead of the tin ones used when Ken's opened. Otherwise, the clam cake making here is essentially unchanged.

Sunday is the biggest day for clam cake sales. "Families come after church. They'll order 10 or 12 with French fries and a side of dill pickles, sit down at a picnic table, and go to town." Dill pickles? Tartar sauce, catsup, and mustard are more common. But the first bite of a Ken's clam cake explains. It's fresh, crispy, perfectly fried, and chock full of clams but bland for lack of seasoning.

"Try it with the tartar," Wilcox encourages, as if anticipating this reaction. And, in fact, Ken's homemade tarter is distinguished by an abundance of crisp, tart pickle bits—the perfect accompaniment.

Why do so few Maine restaurants go for this kind of clam cake gold by making their own?

Wilcox thinks it's because "people are used to their clam cakes being made a certain way," either at a restaurant their family has always gone to or at home. "They're not going to be satisfied with a clam cake that's different."

Including a lot of people who couldn't imagine eating any clam cake but his.

Common Accompaniments to Clam Cakes in Maine

In order of acceptability/popularity: Ketchup, dill pickles, tartar sauce, and, less frequently, mustard. (In fact, in the late 1980s, Harmon's clam cake company sold its own Mother's brand of mustard.)

>> If the line is too long at Ken's, drive two minutes down Route 9 to **The Clambake Restaurant** (354 Pine Point Rd., Scarborough, ME, 207-883-4871, theclambake.com). Odds are at least one of their almost 900 seats will be available. Yes, The Clambake is a seafoodery for the masses, from its self-serve ordering and pickup windows to its four cavernous dining rooms and big outdoor tented picnic area. That tent has the million-dollar view of a salt marsh but don't go out there until you've at least checked out the museum of natural history that is the Prouts Neck dining room, with its displays of real taxidermy animals that are neither from the sea nor, in some cases, Maine. Clambake founder Donald Thurlow's 2004 obituary says he enjoyed hunting and fishing, and I've got to just assume these are his trophies because the current owners are not talking. The manager on duty the quiet early fall day I visited answered questions about the clam cakes and how they're made with a chilly, "Yes, they're homemade. But we're not going to give you the recipe." Judging from their cake's unusual but not altogether unpleasant sweetness—this is the clam cake that most resembles a fried Twinkie—I'd be willing to bet one stuffed raccoon that 1. this is their recipe and 2. sugar is one ingredient in it that they could also stand to add to their corporate personality.

LOBSTER SHACK AT TWO LIGHTS
225 TWO LIGHTS RD., CAPE ELIZABETH, ME, 207-799-1677, LOBSTERSHACKTWOLIGHTS.COM

It took 45 minutes just to place an order at the Lobster Shack at Two Lights one recent sunny early September afternoon. Mind you, this was *after* Labor Day. One can only imagine the wait on a weekend in July or August.

Which could explain why Two Lights' owners and staff ignored multiple requests for an interview that could generate more business. Why would they want that when they can barely handle the business they have now?

So why are they even in here?

Two reasons:

1. The Lobster Shack at Two Lights' absolutely spectacular oceanfront setting.

2. House-made clam cakes that are among the top two or three in the state.

This is not even to mention their namesake lobster, which has earned them multiple Best Lobster Roll prizes.

This rugged spot near two lighthouses (hence the name) has hosted a seasonal lobster shack since the 1920s and been in the current owners' family since 1968, when Jim Leadbetter and his wife, Ruth, decided that waking up at 3 a.m. to make the doughnuts at their Portland bakery wasn't taxing enough. The Leadbetters expanded the shack's menu to include fried seafood, including clam cakes made from Jim's own recipe.

As made by Jim's descendants today, their clam cakes are cakey but not heavy and sparkle with a light salt garnish, a model of how good a simple food—well and freshly made—can be.

Baker Jim also established Two Lights' reputation for wonderful biscuits and old-fashioned desserts like Grape-Nuts pudding, oatmeal pie (like pecan pie minus the pecans), and strawberry shortcake. These are all now made by his grandson, Jeff Porch, and displayed at the ordering counter to derail your best-laid plans to eat in moderation.

After placing your order and paying, there is more waiting—this time for your number to come over the PA—and two choices of eating spaces. The cozy indoor dining room beside the pickup window is a curiosity shop of antique tools and mismatched furniture and great if it's raining; otherwise, eat outside.

With the water crashing, the wind blowing, the seagulls lurking, and the nearby foghorn sounding, it's wild out there but also breathtakingly beautiful. It's easy to imagine people toting their own food and drink and staying the afternoon, hence the multiple posted signs pleading against it. "Do not feed the seagulls," other signs read. But judging from the lack of signs and people's behavior, climbing and sitting on the rocks amidst the crashing surf is A-OK.

Highroller Lobster in nearby Portland sells what are reportedly quite good lobster rolls at bright red picnic tables meant to mimic the ones here (which should give you an idea of the Lobster Shack at Two Lights' fame). But Highroller does not have clam cakes. And you won't leave there full *and* as satisfyingly wind-weary as the people who pulled the seafood you're enjoying out of the water.

Should You Want to Work Off Some of Your Two Lights Meal . . .

There are two parks quite close to the restaurant. **Two Lights State Park** (7 Tower Dr., Cape Elizabeth, maine.gov/dacf) is on Route 77 less than a mile from the Lobster Shack at Two Lights and has oceanfront views to rival it, as well as about 2 miles of footpaths. But it's actually further away from the eponymous two lighthouses (one of which has been decommissioned).

For an up-close look at the lighthouse made famous by painter Edward Hopper, drive 15 minutes north to the town-owned **Fort Williams Park** (1000 Shore Rd., Cape Elizabeth, portlandheadlight.com). There you can tour the Portland Head lightkeeper's house museum, swim at a small rocky beach, and take yet another picture of *the* most-photographed lighthouse in America.

Harmon's: An Oral History

If you've eaten more than one or two clam cakes outside of your home in Maine, chances are that you've eaten Harmon's. They are the one and only company that still makes clam cake products for restaurants, clam shacks, and home cooks that don't make their own, and they are popular.

The company has its origins in a Scarborough, Maine, restaurant known for its clam cakes and fried clams. A former innkeeper in the Higgins Beach summer cottage village he helped develop, Ed Higgins opened the Conora restaurant in 1945, creating the name by combining parts of the names of his wife Ora and daughter Constance.

But local historian Rodney Laughton says it was the second generation of the restaurant's family ownership—Constance and her husband, Lawrence Harmon—who introduced the clam cakes and made them famous.

Constance's granddaughter, Bonnie Jorde, worked at the restaurant as a teenager and picks up the story from there.

"It wasn't a fancy place, but they had standards. I remember my grandfather wouldn't start cooking the entree until people had finished their appetizer or salad. He was very strict like that.

"My grandfather would go down to the docks to get fresh clams. They made huge, huge vats of clam cake and fried clam batter every night. . . . They also had Indian pudding and Jell-O salads and everything was freshly prepared. . . .

"My grandmother said, 'People are always asking for the [clam cake] recipe. If they only knew!'"

Jorde interpreted this to mean her grandmother got it from a cookbook or some other commonly available source. Jorde remembers

Harmon's story starts with this 1940s restaurant.

times when the lines to get into the restaurant would be 50-people deep, though she said not everyone was there for the clam cakes.

"They were really more famous for the fried clams. . . .

"None of their four kids wanted to take over when my grandparents wanted to retire so they sold the restaurant and the recipes to two men who ran it into the ground. It really dwindled in quality, and then the building was destroyed in a fire."

That was the end of the Conora but not of the clam cakes. The Harmons had retained the rights to the restaurant's catering arm and passed it along to daughter Jean Burdwood.

At first, Burdwood just continued Conora's church supper and fair business, but in 1984, she partnered with friend Rae Bacon to start freezing clam cakes for sale in restaurants and supermarkets under the Harmon's name, thus greatly expanding the brand's reach and renown.

By the early aughts, Burdwood and Bacon were ready to retire and put the business up for sale. Enter Steve Liautaud, a Chicago restaurateur newly relocated to Maine.

"I was flipping burgers at a soccer cookout at my kid's school alongside another parent who owned the Clam Shack in Kennebunk, and he told me about this little company in Windsor, Maine, that made clam cakes that was [up for sale]. He said he sold a ton of them. I called [Burdwood and Bacon] on a Thursday, and they said, 'Let's have lunch on Friday.'"

Liautaud had never had a Maine clam cake. But he learned quickly.

"It was basically a cheaper version of the fried clam experience, made with scraps of clam, a product of that Yankee instinct to stretch money as far as you can that a lot of people loved. Kids liked it better than fried clams, and the elderly could chew it. It was really popular with the really young and the really old. . . .

"The price was astronomical, so no one had made an offer."

Liautaud offered less but said it could be cash and quick, which appealed to the women.

"They had 18 customers at the time, but they had announced that they were going out of business. I said, 'I want to talk to all 18 customers. If they're still on board, I'm in.'

"I started calling. People said, 'Oh my God, it's been a nightmare—it'd be awesome if you bought it.' . . . These women didn't even have voicemail. People were knocking on windows at their house trying to order. But people loved the product so much they put up with it because they were the only ones that made the thing. . . .

"I sold $50,000 worth of product in that one morning. I told [Burdwood and Bacon] I'd buy it providing they taught me how to make it so I could fill those orders. They said, 'Fine.'"

For the next 30 days, this twenty-first-century big-city businessman learned how to run a small-town food business as if it were 1930.

"The recipe has egg yolks. They'd buy cases and cases and cases of eggs. And this one woman would stand there all night long separating the whites from the yolks. I said, 'You know you can buy egg yolks already separated and pasteurized.' They weren't aware."

Similarly, Liautaud said, another woman spent her days sticking labels on the plain white boxes they used to sell the clam cakes in supermarkets, instead of having boxes with pictures and information printed.

"They'd freak out when they got calls from Rhode Island, or from someone who wanted them to ship overseas. They didn't trust it. . . . They were making a good living in a cash business, and they wanted to go to bingo on Thursday or to bowl on Tuesday. . . .

"They didn't weigh anything, which created consistency problems. When I asked Jean how much of a certain ingredient they used, she'd say, 'A handful.' That's how they rolled."

Still, he liked the women. The feeling was mutual.

"At the end of the 30 days, they told me: 'It was never about the money. It was about saving the family name and taking it to the next level, and the second you walked in, we knew you were the guy.'"

Liautaud did modernize and expand Harmon's business to out-of-state and non-traditional locations like gas station convenience stores, but he continued the women's tradition of selling at county fairs—something he grew to love.

"I bought Harmon's as a business. But then I'd meet someone at a fair who was 70 years old who would choke up telling me how Harmon's was always the first stop when she used to come to the fair with her grandpa and dad, and I realized that I was really a steward of a part of the fabric of this area. It was a 180-degree shift in my thinking."

The physical demands of the fair work and the increasing difficulty of sourcing clams affordably led to Liautaud's decision to sell in 2019. But he looks back on his Harmon's experience fondly.

"It was an amazing 13 years."

Harmon's is now owned and run by Chris Johnson, his wife, Michele Bowman, and his sister, Sadye Clark, from a white corrugated building on the industrial outskirts of Portland. There at Harmon's headquarters—really just a big open room—employees blend, form, and fry before handing their clam and crab cakes off to the cold storage company next door.

Johnson and Bowman both previously worked in his family's wholesale lobster and bait business. The trio bought Harmon's at auction only a little more than four months before the start of the pandemic.

Bowman: "Before the pandemic, two-thirds of our sales were to restaurants. So when COVID hit, our sales dropped in half. . . . So we tried to pivot more to our retail [supermarket] business. But we needed more retail boxes. And the company we had been using was backed up with orders for COVID test kits. We had product, but nothing to sell it in."

Why did they buy Harmon's?

Johnson: "Number one, we thought it was scalable. Number two, because of the brand identity. . . . People our age and older know Harmon's."

Bowman: "We've got some hard-core fans from the fixed-income crowd. Like this guy from upstate New York named Robert Mitchell.

He calls every three or four months and says, 'This is Robert Mitchell from upstate New York. I need another seven boxes.' We've saved some of the voicemails: They make us smile."

Johnson: "We thought if we could clean it up and ran it a little differently, there was lots of potential."

Bowman (nodding): "We thought it could be changed for the better."

And they have made changes, like switching from a hamburger former to cookie dough dropper to apportion the dough. They've also expanded clam-cake-product offerings to include raw clam cake dough for restaurants to form and fry themselves. And they've turned previous owner Steve Liautaud's lone crab cake offering into a four-product line.

Johnson: "Volume-wise, it's 80 percent clam cakes, but they make up only 60 to 70 percent of revenue. Plus, everyone knows what a crab cake is."

They also stopped doing fairs and festivals. The Harmon's fair trailer now sits idle in the factory parking lot.

Bowman: "Steve really enjoyed his interactions with consumers. But we'd rather make friends with distributors than the public. That's what's good for business."

Some Places Serving Harmon's: Becky's Diner, Portland; Bob's Clam Hut, Kittery; Cape Pier Chowder, Cape Porpoise; Clam Shack, Kennebunk; Harraseeket Lunch & Lobster Company, South Freeport; Maine Diner, Wells; Rapid Ray's, Saco; Red's Eats, Wiscasset; Sea Basket, Wiscasset; Sprague's Lobster, Wiscasset.

Retail packages of Harmon's are also available at Maine fish stores and supermarkets, including Shaw's, Big Y, and Market Basket and out-of-state through mainelobsternow.com.

Beaches Near the Cakes in Maine

Unless otherwise noted, fees are parking for nonresidents in the summer.

Higgins Beach, 41 Ocean Ave., Scarborough. Popular surfing beach; swimmers should beware of rocks. $15.

Old Orchard Beach, 2 Old Orchard St., Old Orchard. The big kahuna of area beaches, complete with boardwalk and amusement park. Area parking from free to $20, depending on how far you're willing to walk.

Pine Point Beach, 30–26 Ave. 5, Scarborough. Four miles of white sand beach adjacent to Old Orchard but lots quieter. $5 per car before 9 a.m./$15 after.

Scarborough Beach State Park, 418 Black Point Park, Scarborough. Very popular soft, sandy beach with food trucks, surfing, and swimming in warm water (by Maine standards, anyway). $10/adults and $7/children, cash for beach entry (parking free).

VIRGINIA-STYLE CLAM FRITTERS

Looking for crab cakes on the Eastern Shore and nearby Virginia Beach? Tourism websites should do you fine. This part of this book is for people who want to eat the seafood dish locals love. Most of the few restaurants that serve clam fritters on the water in Virginia are small local "joints" where tourists rarely tread. Visitors in search of multiple clam fritter experiences in this area would do well to time their visit to one of the many area fundraising dinners and festivals featuring clam fritters.

BEACH PUB
1001 LASKIN RD., VIRGINIA BEACH, VA, 757-422-8817,
BEACHPUBVB.COM

Want to know what it's like to be famous? Go to the Beach Pub for the first time. All heads will turn, and all minds will be wondering, "Who is *that*?" especially if you make the mistake of sitting at a regular's table.

If you want to fit in, decline a menu and order eggs with double-dipped clam fritters. What you'll get is like the clam pancakes served north of the Bay Bridge-Tunnel but different in having spicy heat and being served as a breakfast side.

Beach Pub owner Dan Whelan says he doesn't know of another restaurant in Virginia Beach that serves clam fritters of any kind—never mind ones that are griddled *and* flash-fried half the time—and a Web search confirms it. Fiery clam fritters are only a tradition in the Barco family that owns this locally famous family-style seafooder a mile from the city's namesake oceanfront.

Beach Pub founder Buddy Barco grew up only a few hundred feet from Virginia Beach's Cape Henry Lighthouse, the son of a volunteer Life-Saving Service member who died when his son was eight. To help out his widowed mom, young Buddy would hunt, fish, and forage for food to feed the family, including clams she used to make Tabasco-spiked clam fritters.

A grown-up Buddy put that dish on the Beach Pub's 1978 opening menu, alongside oysters Rockefeller, clams Barco (like clams casino), and fish hash. It was those old-fashioned favorites and the Pub's commitment to from-scratch cooking (Barco's daughter, Suzy Whelan, was making potato salad at 8:30 a.m. one recent morning) that piqued the interest of *Diners, Drive-Ins and Dives*, resulting in a 2011 segment that has attracted the tourists.

Barco died in 2019, and the Beach Pub is now owned and run by his daughters and their husbands with help from Barco's 81-year-old former business partner, Harry Smithson, and his 87-year-old widow, Shirley (he does prep work; she bakes desserts), with few changes.

That includes the space, which is as old-fashioned as the food and the subject of some Yelp griping. Whelan shrugs it off by saying, "This is a place you can bring your kids and not worry about it." Wall decorations are a dense blend of sports, Virginia Beach, and Barco family memorabilia, including a mounted red cup Buddy used to disguise his Scotch drinking. Now on Christmas Eve, everyone in the restaurant gets a red cupful of their favorite poison and toasts the late owner.

"It's too bad you didn't get to meet him," Whelan says at one point. But spending time in his restaurant with his family, friends, and fritters, you almost feel like you have.

CAPTAIN E'S HURRICANE GRILL AND TIKI BAR
9104 STARLING CREEK RD., SAXIS, VA, 757-854-0807

Chincoteague is a famously family-friendly vacation spot.

What to do if you want to eat Eastern Shore clam fritters and party?

Go to Captain E's, a seafood restaurant and bar on the water in Saxis far away from the ponies and kiddies.

You need to navigate around Captain E's mobile trailer to find the entrance to the squat building that opens into a dark bar and a small dining room with a door leading to the beach and a second bar, this one tiki-themed. That's if you get to Captain E's by car; on weekends in the summer, half of the customers arrive by boat, and the place rocks.

But mid-afternoon on a showery spring day it was quiet enough for the chef to be able to come out and talk clam fritters.

"Joy's the chef. I just do odd cookin'," J. D. Marshall corrects. A former butcher who hails from nearby Greenbackville, he's also in charge of maintenance—"I made this booth we're sitting in," he says proudly—monitors the soft-shell crabs that are shedding in wooden tanks on one side of the restaurant's driveway, and developed Captain E's clam fritter recipe.

"The biggest two complaints about clam fritters are one, there's not enough clam and two, they're too greasy." Marshall says it took him three years to create a recipe that gets around those problems, and "I'm not going to just give it away."

But he was willing to speak about his fritters generally, revealing that he does deep fry "but I brown them on a griddle first to keep the grease from soaking in."

He deals with the first problem—of not enough clams—by using a quart of clams per gallon batch and by stacking two thin patties on every clam fritter sandwich. "That pretty much guarantees a clam in every bite."

Other Captain E menu highlights include "bites" made with soft crab, drum or rockfish, fried oysters, baked ham and oysters, peas and dumplings, and crabby fries (like a crab version of the Canadian poutine).

The previously referenced Joy Bardinelli is not just the chef but also owner of Captain E's with her husband, Frank. He helped open Pizza Huts up and down the East Coast; she once worked for Taco Bell. Then Hurricane

Sandy leveled the commercial fishing operation her father, Arnold Ray Evans (i.e., Captain E), previously ran on this site.

Says Bardinelli: "All that was left was mud and nets. While we were cleaning up, I said, 'Daddy, this might be the time to do the restaurant we've been talking about.' Five years later, we opened."

Now the Bardinellis get to run a restaurant their way, the right way to Marshall's way of thinking. "We spend all day Wednesday and Thursday prepping for the weekend. We could just go to Cisco," he points out.

The family's commercial fishery heritage gives them access to the freshest seafood available, like the soft shell crabs Marshall walks across the driveway, and oysters from private fishing grounds when the usual suppliers are dry.

And when Captain E's can't find someone selling local clams for the clam fritters, "I've gone out clamming myself," says Marshall. "How many chefs"—or cooks—"do that?"

EXMORE DINER
4264 MAIN ST., EXMORE, VA, 757-442-4313

Most of the authentic diners still in business in America are struggling.

Waning interest in their old-fashioned eats combined with the cost of old-building upkeep and competition from big-pocketed chains makes it hard for these twentieth-century eateries to make it in the twenty-first.

The Exmore Diner is one happy exception. Despite a location a third of a mile from one of the area's few McDonald's, it hosted a steady stream of customers one recent weekday well after peak lunch hour, even as waitresses took turns grabbing the ringing phone to answer questions about the day's specials.

What's their secret? A menu small by diner standards featuring old-fashioned and

Both diner and fritter fans flock to the Exmore's shiny chrome door.

regional favorites like creamed chipped beef and scrapple egg sandwiches and lots of fresh, local seafood in dishes like clam fritters. In fact, the Exmore Diner was the only restaurant to make the Eastern Shore of Virginia Tourism Commission's 2020 local's choice list of best clam fritters. (The other winners were local firemen's festivals—see p. 18.)

"I don't think that many restaurants make clam fritters," says diner owner Evelyn Pruitt, declining the invitation to brag. And Pruitt is not quite sure why. "They're not a hassle to make. And compared to other seafood, the price is not high."

Pruitt grew up eating her mother's clam fritters, and her diner makes them the way she likes: pan (instead of deep) fried, thin and crispy, and filled with chopped local Willis Wharf clams, bellies included. Asked about the local tradition of belly inclusion, which speckle the fritters with black, Pruitt said, "I once made clam chowder without the bellies: It was the plainest chowder I ever had in my life."

Customers can buy clam fritters on a roll, on a plate, or as part of the diner's popular two-seafoods-and-two-sides special. Old-fashioned sides include fried apples, succotash, stewed tomatoes, turnip greens, and corn and limas. The Exmore is also known for its homemade soups and seasonal offerings like soft shell crab, drum and drum ribs, and swelling toad.

"We clean the soft shells really well," Pruitt says of the crab. Drum ribs are a form of drum fish that you can pick up and eat like baby backs. Swelling toad isn't a toad at all but rather a puffy fish that tastes like sea bass. It's also eaten out-of-hand, in this case like a chicken drumstick, which is why it's sometimes called "chicken of the sea." (Anything would be better than swelling toad!)

The building is another draw. This 1945, 44-seat Silk City was built and located in New Jersey until local produce trucker Preston Kellam spotted it for sale on his way to a Yankees game in 1953 and moved it to its current location. Pruitt was a waitress and manager at the diner before buying it in 1991. She's run it with the help of various family members, including son Sean Hart and his wife, Crystal, ever since.

Diners have always been most common in the urban Northeast, where most were made, but unaltered ones are even becoming rare there. Architectural historian and diner fan Marc Wagner enthuses over the Exmore's "wonderful multicolor tile" and original stools, wood trim, and booths, saying it adds up to one the most "exquisite diner interiors" in the state.

Pruitt accepts the compliment with a laugh. "There's a lot broken in here, believe me!"

Smith Island Cake Is a Multi-Layered Thing

Like a little cake with your frosting? Then you'll love Smith Island cake, a yellow cake traditional to that Chesapeake Bay island with fudgy chocolate frosting between every one of its seven-to-ten layers.

Women living on the island as far back as the late 1600s supposedly made this torte-like treat for their hard-working fisherman husbands, for whom the cake's 708 calories and 30 grams of fat was not a big problem.

It was made on the island—and pretty much only on the island—until renowned island cook Frances E. Kitching put a recipe for the cake in the 1994 edition of her popular *Mrs. Kitching's Smith Island Cookbook*. Further spreading its fame: Being named Maryland's official dessert in 2008 following cake deliveries to every single sitting state legislator.

Now many Eastern Shore restaurants and bakeries in Maryland and Virginia feature the cake, both in the original flavor combination and new and exciting variations like strawberry, lemon, and coconut. Becca's bakery of Melfa, Virginia, supplies the Exmore Diner.

Making the cake is more time-consuming than difficult: The hardest part is handling the thin cake layers without having them break. That, and not having it totally wreck your diet.

Smith Island Cake

Cake

Recipe for your favorite yellow cake or 1 box yellow cake mix (yielding 2 8-inch layers)

Icing

2 cups granulated sugar

1 cup evaporated milk

6 ounces unsweetened chocolate

6 tablespoons unsalted butter

2 teaspoons vanilla extract

For the cake: Preheat oven to 350°F. Generously grease and flour 2 or 3 8-inch cake pans, then line bottom with parchment paper. Prepare cake batter. Pour ⅛ of the batter (about ⅔ cup) into each pan, and then spread it evenly to the edges of each pan with the back of a spoon or a spatula. Bake until the edges are browned and the cake is completely cooked, about 10 to 12 minutes. Let cake cool on a rack for 5 minutes, then run a knife around the perimeter of the pan to loosen cake and invert it on a rack. Clean and refill the pans and cook until you have 8 cooled layers.

For the icing: In a medium saucepan, stir sugar and evaporated milk together over low heat until warm. Add chocolate and simmer until melted. Add butter and bring to a boil over medium heat. Boil for 12 to 15 minutes, stirring as needed. Add vanilla. Frosting will be thin and glossy. Let icing sit for about 30 minutes, or until it is thick enough to spread. Place about ¼ cup of frosting on the top of each layer and frost to edges. Let cake cool in the refrigerator for 30 minutes before frosting the sides of the cake and then, finally, the top.

Yield: 10 to 12 servings

MARTHA'S KITCHEN
19423 SAXIS RD., SAXIS, VA, 757-709-1658

"The devil's on the warpath," says Martha Linton of Martha's Kitchen, by way of explaining why her glasses are missing a lens.

I was there for her signature gargantuan clam fritters, but first came the story of how she had broken her glasses, lost her upper false teeth, and fell and hit her head on the bathroom floor early that morning. She takes the lens out of her pocket to prove it.

You've heard of people who can cook so well they can do it with their eyes closed? Well, Martha can cook blurry, while telling you a million stories.

That makes a visit to Martha's Kitchen more like having a meal cooked by an aunt or grandmother than eating at a restaurant. And this is not just true on days when she breaks her glasses, judging by the Yelp reviews.

Linton, 71, has been serving breakfast and lunch in this barebones little space in the fishing village of Saxis for "15 years too long," is how she puts it.

She was running a bait and tackle business nearby when local fishermen began asking her to make them lunch. "So I would run home and make them sandwiches, until I got into a fight with my brother, and he turned me in to the health department. They said, 'You don't have a license for making sandwiches.' So I started making fried chicken, until my other brother got mad at me and turned me in for that," she says with a grin.

Good thing the restaurant space across the street became available or Linton might be making license plates instead of fritters.

Linton has warmed up the cinderblock building with wooden booths and inspirational religious signs like "Let go and let God." Though it sits right on the Saxis dock, the restaurant has never flooded during Linton's "too-long" time. Not even during Hurricane Sandy. "You know why? I prayed," she says.

No wonder the chalkboard menu looks so cheery. It lists egg dishes for breakfast and soft crab and crab cake sandwiches for lunch but her clam fritters are the profile picture on Martha's Kitchen's Facebook page and among her proudest culinary creations.

Though her recipe is Eastern Shore standard (eggs, clams, onion, and pancake mix combined and cooked on a grill), producing the usual clam pancake, the size is anything but normal. Inspired by a cook at a now-defunct

Chincoteague restaurant, Linton's fritters are as big as your head, or more than double the typical, a disparity rendered ridiculous by the way she serves them: as a sandwich on a standard burger bun.

Who are her customers?

"In the morning, I'm the local hangout for has-been watermen," some "as tight as wax," she complains. "They'll buy a cup of coffee and think they're doing you a favor." The lunch crowd is mainly tourists, sent there by Chincoteague motelers and tourism people aware that a meal at Martha's is at least as interesting—for most people, probably more—than looking at ponies.

Beaches Near the Fritters in Virginia

Fees are parking for nonresidents in the summer.

Assateague Island National Seashore, 11800 Marsh View Ln., Berlin, Maryland. Twin public beaches in pony country. South Ocean Beach has a smaller parking lot and so is not as crowded, but North Ocean Beach has more amenities. $20.

Cape Charles Beach, Bay Ave., Cape Charles, Virginia. Free public beach in quaint, touristy Cape Charles. As popular for kayaking, paddle boarding, and bird watching as for sunbathing and calm-water swimming.

Virginia Beach, 2100 Parks Ave., Virginia Beach. State's premiere beach known for its long coastline, boardwalk, restaurants, entertainment, and tourists. Street and garage parking for about $10.

Index of Clam Cake/Fritter Places by Features

- Arrive by boat: Cap'n Jack's, Captain E's, Chelo's Waterfront, Evelyn's, Jim's Dock, N.O. Clam Bar

- Featured on *Diners, Drive-Ins and Dives*: Anthony's, Aunt Carrie's, Beach Pub, Evelyn's

- Waiter/waitress service: Aunt Carrie's, Beach Pub, Cap'n Jack's, Captain E's, Chelo's Waterfront, Evelyn's, Exmore Diner, George's, Hitching Post, Iggy's (Warwick), Jim's Dock, Martha's Kitchen, Summer Shack, Quito's

- Water views: Aunt Carrie's, Blount Clam Shack on the Waterfront, Cap'n Jack's, Captain E's, Champlin's, Clambake, Evelyn's, Flo's, George's, Iggy's (Warwick), Jim's Dock, Lobster Shack, Lobster Shack at Two Lights, Monahan's, Quito's, Sea Swirl, Sea View, Tony's, Woodman's

- Year-round: Amaral's, Anthony's, Beach Pub, Blount Clam Shack and Market, Cap'n Jack's, Champlin's, Egg Roll Lady, Exmore Diner, George's, Martha's Kitchen, Summer Shack, Woodman's, Ye Olde English Fish & Chips

3
CELEBRATING CLAM CAKES AND FRITTERS

Many foods are delicious—but only a few are part of a citizenry's identity—so beloved that they're the draw for nonprofit fundraisers and the focus of an annual tasting crawl. Also, the foundation of a gift shop's product line, a cartoonist's career, and a widely popular national TV show.

Clam cakes and their quahog base are these kinds of special foods as you can read and see in the following sections.

THE TV SHOW

Clam cakes have received their due on the expected, important food and travel websites like *Saveur, National Geographic,* and Food52. But none of these stories rivaled the importance of the spotlight cakes and quahogs have received on the prime-time cartoon *Family Guy.*

The first mention came early on, in the fourth episode of the show's first season, when the show's dim-witted namesake paternus Peter Griffin, looking for food to serve in his new basement bar, turns to his wife, Lois, and says, "Hey, honey, you know those little clam cakes you make whenever we have company? I need about a dozen. Actually, better make it like 600."

The second was in the lyrics to a song the family's debonair dog, Brian, and disturbed baby, Stewie, sang with Frank Sinatra Jr. in a 2006 nod to the Rat Pack: "We go together there's no mistake, like a bowl of chowder and a big clam cake."

There is also the memorable fourth-season episode where all the male members of the Griffin family take EpiCat to see who can go the longest without throwing up. Just as the ensuing pukefest seems to be winding down, Lois shows up with a big steaming pot of chowder, and the throwing up resumes. (Though no clam cakes are in sight, they are the usual accompaniment to chowder.)

This is not to mention that the show is set in a town named after the variety of clam originally favored for clam cakes and that Quahog residents' favorite bar is called the Drunken Clam.

These are only the most clam-centric of hundreds of Rhode Island references on *Family Guy* that can be credited (or blamed) on Danny Smith, a long-tenured *Family Guy* writer-producer who grew up in the state. Smith has fond memories of his annual field trip to Rocky Point with fellow Roman Catholic altar boys that always ended with the supposed little "angels" lobbing clam cakes at one another in a giant Shore Dinner Hall fried food fight.

Show creator Seth MacFarlane attended the Rhode Island School of Design and immediately picked up on Smith's Rhode Island accent while interviewing him for a staff job in 1998. "We started talking about [late Providence Mayor] Buddy Cianci, Haven Brothers [food truck], Del's Lemonade [see p. 68]—all these references we had in common. Then he said, 'You start tomorrow.' We literally bonded over Rhode Island."

And so it follows that when Fox executives told MacFarlane and his writing team that they wanted the new show to be set in a specific region of the country, Smith said, "Dude, it's got to be in Rhode Island!" He further argued for the fictional Quahog, over the name of any

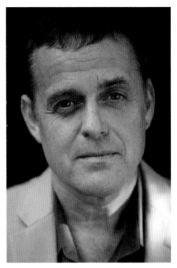

Danny Smith

real RI town. This was based on the local reaction to an unflattering reference Smith made to Pawtucket, Rhode Island, on a previous show—including death threats and a live-on-air phone call from a RI disk jockey at 3 a.m. PST.

"But if we said things people didn't like [on *Family Guy*] about a place that didn't exist, I figured we'd be in the clear."

The strategy seems to be working. Instead of complaining, Smith says, "People are always coming up to me saying, 'Quahog is Cranston, right?' if they live in Cranston, or North Scituate, if that's where they live, like hopefully. And whatever they say, I always answer, 'Yes, yes, that's it.'"

But why call the fictional town Quahog?

Smith says the reason is rooted in two comedy rules: 1. Specific is always funnier than general. That is, quahog is funnier than a generic-sounding place like Springfield (sorry *Simpsons* fans). 2. Words with the K sound are funnier than ones without.

Asked if clam cakes are the funniest of quirky Rhode Island foods, Smith answers, "It certainly does have a lot of Ks."

THE TV CHEF

Emeril Lagasse is the most famous chef to ever come out of Southern New England. But he very nearly became a drummer instead.

Long before he became a Food Network star, Lagasse was such an accomplished percussionist that he was offered a full scholarship to the prestigious New England Conservatory in Boston. But he turned that down to instead enroll in the then-fledgling culinary arts program at Johnson & Wales

University in Providence, Rhode Island. He grew up in nearby Fall River, Massachusetts, helping his Portuguese-American mother in the kitchen.

In addition to helping the Food Network figure out what makes a successful cooking show and bringing "Bam" back into common usage for the first time since *The Flintstones*, Lagasse introduced local culinary oddities like chow mein sandwiches, stuffies, clear clam chowder, salmon pie, and, of course, clam cakes, to a national audience.

Lagasse first experienced fish-flavored dough balls eating his mom's salt cod fritters. (Salt cod is a salted and dried version of this historically important New England fish used in many Portuguese-American dishes.)

In his 2015 cookbook *Essential Emeril*, the chef writes of his early memories eating clam cakes at Rocky Point in Providence. And about how "when I ate beignets for the first time in New Orleans," the city where Lagasse established his culinary bona fides, "I immediately thought of my childhood clam cakes and wondered how I could give beignets a savory turn."

Lagasse has been riffing on this dish ever since. Among the many variations showing up in his restaurants, cookbooks, TV shows, and website: shrimp and zucchini, pumpkin and corn, crab and corn, black-eyed pea, conch and beer batter crab fritters, blue crab hush puppies, crabmeat, and crawfish and corn beignets, and, yes, also good ol' clam cakes—though they're hardly plain.

In almost all cases, Lagasse "kicks" the traditional, bland Rocky Point-style cake "up a notch" with non-traditional add-ins like garlic, onion, scallion, cayenne, and hot sauce.

Emeril is especially partial to an eggplant variation on his crab and corn fritter because of the way the eggplant "almost melts right into the batter." Make it by substituting one large globe eggplant (diced into small pieces, sprinkled with salt and Creole seasoning and either sautéed in olive oil or oven roasted until tender) and half-inch pieces of roasted red pepper and fresh basil (both to taste) for the corn and crabmeat in the crab and corn fritter recipe at emerils.com.

Celebrity Watch

- Tony-, Emmy-, and Academy-award-winning actress Viola Davis spoke about "having to have clam cakes and fried clams" on visits back to her native Rhode Island in a 2014 interview in *Rhode Island Monthly* magazine.
- Clam cakes were first on the list of "Rhode Island things we miss" *Dumb and Dumber* filmmaker Peter Farrelly talked about in an interview he and his brother/collaborator Bob did with Collider.com in 2011. (Del's was second.)

- Despite her financial/family interest in several Rhode Island restaurants, including the Back Forty in North Kingstown and Union & Main in East Greenwich, actress, model, and former Miss Universe Olivia Culpo once recommended readers of the UK's *Daily Mail* get clam cakes at Iggy's (perhaps because her restaurants don't serve them).

- Clam cakes are a symbol of assimilation in "Mrs. Sen," a story in Jhumpa Lahiri's 2000 Pulitzer Prize-winning collection *Interpreter of Maladies*. In several scenes, Lahiri contrasts the clam cakes she knew from growing up in South County, Rhode Island, with the raw fresh fish Mrs. Sen is always buying to make dishes that remind her of her Indian homeland. And when Mrs. Sen first has clam cakes, she "put a good deal of Tabasco sauce and black pepper" on them to make them more—"Like pakoras, no?" her husband asks.

- Among the celebrities who have eaten at Flo's in Middletown, Rhode Island, judging from the memorabilia that now decorate the walls: trumpeter Chuck Mangione, the Blues Brothers, Foreigner, and comedian/talk show host Dennis Miller.

- The Cardi brothers of Cardi's Furniture & Mattresses recently used clam cakes to promote the storage space in one of their sectional sofas. In a local TV ad that ran in early 2022, Ron and Pete Cardi are lounging on a sofa when an employee comes by and takes a tray of clam cakes out of one of the couch's cubbies and hands it to Pete. Sure, featuring clam cakes in an ad for a dining room set would have made a lot more sense, but the main reason the brothers are celebrities in Southern New England (and sell so much furniture there) is because their ads are so homespun and goofy.

- Captain Frosty's in Dennis, Massachusetts, has fed actor Ethan Hawke, singer Steve Tyler, mystery writer Mary Higgins Clark, and many actors who have played the nearby Cape Playhouse (including Fannie Flagg and Lee Remick).

- Oscar-nominated actor Richard Jenkins (*The Visitor*, *The Shape of Water*) rhapsodized about Aunt Carrie's in the *New Yorker* in 2020. "It's this great seafood restaurant," the Rhode Island resident said. "You can sit indoors, because all the windows are open and the sea breeze is blowing." In fact, Jenkins celebrated his 51st wedding anniversary at Aunt Carrie's the day before sitting for the interview.

THE SONG

Those upset about the lack of clams in Rhode Island clam cakes had an ally in late local singer-songwriter Jon Campbell.

A longtime instrumentalist for both Irish and traditional American bands, Campbell wrote his lament about getting "no clams" in "One Clam Cake" shortly after launching his solo career in the mid-1980s.

His Rhode Island Music Hall of Fame entry describes Campbell as a sharp-eyed chronicler of coastal Rhode Island, who wrote about "regional cuisine, swamp Yankees, commercial fishing, politics and local history" with humor or poignancy or (as with his classic, "Keep on Fishin'") both. "One Clam Cake" is on Campbell's 2000 *Keep on Fishin'* album.

Marina Campbell calls "One Clam Cake" one of her dad's wackiest songs and also, likely not coincidentally, one of his most popular. He usually performed it as a sing-along with local audiences who understood its complexity.

Though superficially commiserating with the little man's disappointment with his clamless clam cake, he is a *little* man who is clueless that "it's mostly batter . . . now what's the matter? You must be from Johnston or Silver Lake"—that is, from inland, and uninformed—"if you think you get a clam in one clam cake."

Campbell usually introduced the song by confiding how many Rhode Island clam shacks save money by tying a clam to a piece of string and dragging it through their clam cake batter as a flavoring agent. "The only way you would get a clam is if the string were to let go," he explained, in this setup to the song's last verse and chorus, which ended with Campbell's Louie Armstrong impression. You can do a Jon Campbell impression with the below lyrics and chords.

"One Clam Cake"
By Jon Campbell

Em   D   C7   B7   Em   D   C7   B7
A little man he was very sad, one clam cake was all he had
  Em   D   C7   B7
He heard this voice, it made him shake,
B7   C7   B7
It said, "You get no clam in one clam cake."
          (Chorus)
    Em   D   C7   B7
One clam cake, none in the middle,
Em   D   C7   B7
One clam cake, come on and answer me this riddle
     Em   D   C7   B7
If you pass that clam shack and hit that brake,

B7   C7   B7
Are you gonna get some clam in your clam cake?
         Em   D   C7   B7
One clam cake, ooh, ooh
         Em   D   C7   B7
One clam cake, ooh, ooh.
Well, a little man, he went to Galilee
Just to get a half dozen down by the sea
He didn't want a burger, and he didn't want steak
He just wanted clam in his clam cake.
One clam cake, it's mostly batter
One clam cake, now what's the matter?
You must be from Johnston or Silver Lake,
If you think you get a clam in one clam cake.
One clam cake, ooh, ooh
One clam cake, ooh, ooh.
It's just a quahog cruller, but that says a lot
It'll bust your belly and it'll stop up your heart.
You can mix them in a bowl with some aluminum foil
And you're scoopin' and a scoopin' and boil 'em in oil.
One clam cake, ooh they're effervescent
One clam cake, you know they're practically fluorescent!
Wanna eat something to make your belly ache?
It's like a deep-fried hand grenade, that clam cake.
One clam cake, they're nice and greasy
One clam cake, you'd think it would be easy.
You might get lucky and the string might break
And you might get the clam in your clam cake.
One clam cake, ooh, ooh
One clam cake, ooh, ooh
And when you've got a clam cake, "What a wonderful world!"

THE CRAWL

How many clam cakes can one person eat without barfing? At least a dozen, although after eating seven in an hour, you start "sweating fryolator oil."

That's one of Renee Bessette's takeaways from eight years of Lil Rhody Clam Cake Crawling. An unofficial year-by-year history of this annual day-long clamathon culled from Bessette's Only in Lil Rhody blog follows.

February 2013: Outraged over a Rhode Island state legislator's efforts to make calamari the official state appetizer, Joe Mecca's Big Mouth podcasters Bessette and Joe Mecca argue that the honor really belongs to the more unique, beloved, and locally debated clam cakes. But working their big mouths is all they do until . . .

August 25, 2014: Bessette, Mecca, and Mecca's wife, Carol, known collectively as the Clamarati, crisscross the state to test and rate clam cakes at 12 Rhode Island clam cake spots with the goal of identifying the state's best. Scoring criteria include number of "nubbins" (the Clamarati's name for protruding fried appendages), clam-to-cake ratio, and the serving shack's overall "clambiance" (water view, nautical knick-knacks, etc.). And the winner was? Aunt Carrie's.

August 22, 2015: The trio is back visiting 12 more shacks, including Blount's in Warren. After admiring their lobster bicycle rack and their clam cakes (at least somewhat), a yacht rock guitarist starts playing, and Bessette is outta there.

At the sixth stop at Aunt Carrie's, Joe declares, "I think we should just call it a day." They actually go on to taste six more cakes, but his words are prophetic: Aunt Carrie's wins again.

June 18, 2016: First-time crawler and clam cake visionary Don H. adds a new element to the cake evaluations, finding a fish, a walrus, and Mickey Mouse in nubbin-rich offerings from Macray's, Samantha's Seafood, and Anthony's, respectively. The group's enjoyment of Seafood Haven's clam cakes is marred by the sighting of a dead fish out back. Bessette's comment on Aunt Carrie's: "Like eating a g-d cloud." Nevertheless, the numbers give it to Quito's.

Crawl cofounder Joe Mecca displays the nubbins that have helped make Aunt Carrie's a perennial Crawl champ.

June 24, 2017: After years of ignoring marketing professional Bessette's pleas for press coverage, the *Providence Journal* and *Narragansett Times* both publish crawl stories. This year in Rhode Island, only Mr. Potato Head is more famous. The Clamarati rent a minivan, dubbed the Clam Barge, to accommodate additional tasters, including *Rhode Island Clam Shacks* authors Christopher Scott Martin and David Norton Stone. Three different crawlers' comments on Tommy's: "A bit salty." "Salty." "Very salty." Aunt Carrie's loses again, this time to the Hitching Post (for its garden setting and "soft interior").

June 30, 2018: A Chihuahua called Clambina joins the tasting team. Last year's extensive press coverage jeopardizes the crawlers' clamonymity for any owner not already suspicious of 13 people with clipboards. The day's edible sculptures include one snowman and one turkey. One glass-half-fuller exalts at finding sand in her cake: "Real deal clams!" Aunt Carrie's wins.

June 22, 2019: This year's Rorschach clam shack report includes two dinosaurs and one pair of conjoined twins. Crawler cake comments: on Salty's Landing, "[Late namesake broadcaster] Salty Brine would weep"; George's, "A hundred seagulls can't be wrong!"; and Iggy's, "Much-improved by dipping in Aunt Carrie's blueberry pie." And the winner is? Aunt Carrie's again.

July 10, 2021: After a year pause for the clamdemic, five vaccinated and masked crawlers hit the road only to give Aunt Carrie's the top prize for the fifth (and final) time (to give someone else a chance). Comments on the Hitching Post, "Like a trip to the botanical garden"; and Chevy's of Wickford, "Cursed . . . [by] the Witches of Eastwick."

August 6, 2022 (during a heat wave): With Aunt Carrie's now "mercenaria emeritus," the top prize goes to 2021 second-place finisher Two Little Fish. Once again, Quito's and the Hitching Post score high and Flo's low (the Tiverton police officer posted by the ordering window notwithstanding). Newcomer Roy Boy's of North Kingstown delivers catsup packets (Is this Virginia?) with its greasy cakes and ends up dead last. First-ever out-of-state stand (Dicky's of Rehoboth, Massachusetts) lands mid-pack.

After eight years, hasn't this group clamquered their original goal? Maybe. But it seems they also do it to have fun with puns and for the clamaraderie (and the free beer from sponsor Narragansett Brewing).

COPYCAT LIL RHODY CLAM CAKE DRIVING TOUR

The Clamarati drive all over Rhode Island in search of the best clam cakes.

The following South County-centered GPS-ready itinerary is less of an ordeal, while still allowing for sampling a great variety of RI-style clam cakes in a single (long, stomach-expanding) afternoon.

Although the 25-mile coastal route can be done in reverse order, starting near the Connecticut border allows you to end on a potential high, with the Clamarati favorite Aunt Carrie's and rival Iggy's. Unless otherwise noted, restaurants have ample parking in their own lots and offer both dine-in and takeout (the latter being more advisable if you want to finish this tour before midnight).

1. Two Little Fish, 300 Atlantic Ave., Westerly. Free parking behind the restaurant and in the lot beside it if you tell the attendant you're eating here.

2. Salty's Clam Shack, 668 Atlantic Ave., Westerly. Takeout only.

3. Hitching Post Restaurant, 5402 Post Rd., Charlestown.

4. N.O. Bar Clam Shack, 523 Charlestown Beach Rd., Charlestown.

5. Jim's Dock, 1175 Succotash Rd., Narragansett. Limited parking in front of Jim's or on nearby streets.

Need a break? Refresh your appetite with a walk or swim at East Matunuck State Beach, 950 Succotash Rd., South Kingstown, located right between Jim's Dock and Cap'n Jack's. Arrive at 2 or 3 p.m., and there might even be room in the state parking lot.

6. Cap'n Jack's, 706 Succotash Rd., Wakefield.

7. Champlin's Seafood Deck, 256 Great Island Rd., Narragansett. Limited parking at the restaurant and in the public lot across the street.

8. George's of Galilee, 250 Sand Hill Cove Rd., Narragansett. Free parking in the lot behind the restaurant or valet (also free) just after it if you time it right. Also in the above-mentioned cross-street public lot.

9. Iggy's, 1151 Point Judith Rd., Narragansett. Takeout only.

10. Aunt Carrie's, 1240 Ocean Rd., Narragansett.

Note that Two Little Fish opens at 11:30 a.m. (as do many of these places) and Iggy's and Aunt Carrie's close at 7 or 8 p.m., or about an hour earlier than the nearby Champlin's and George's, so if you're running late, you might want to switch the order of the last four stands. Lines will be shorter and your trip will take less time if you go on a weekday instead of a weekend (other than a Tuesday, when Aunt Carrie's and several other of these restaurants are closed).

TOUR DE CLAM CAKE

The East Bay Bicycle Path is one of Rhode Island's best off-road bike paths. Following a former railroad line, it features great water views and access to East Bay Rhode Island's best seasonal clam cake shacks.

Two carbo-loading ride options follow. The slightly shorter but technically much easier ride, suitable for families with not-too-young kids, sticks mainly to the path. Only the first 5 miles of the longer, more difficult ride are on the bike path, but it is the path's scenic sweet spot.

The longer ride also includes several bridge crossings (one on the old Mount Hope Bridge, which is narrow and has no shoulder), a couple of tough climbs, and more clam cake stops so is better suited for experienced bikers with big appetites.

Both rides are best done by "active" clam cake fans in groups of four or more. This allows for splitting the cost and calories of the clam cakes, which are usually only sold by the half-dozen or dozen.

Though considering all the energy you will be expending to get to these places, should we even be talking about calories? Only in the sense of how much you'll lose.

FAMILY RIDE

Number of miles: 20 round-trip

Number of clam cake joints: 3

Net calories (consumed minus expended, with Del's stop and assuming one clam cake per stop): -300

Terrain: flat

Park: Rose Larisa Park (753–779 Bullocks Point Ave., Riverside) parking lot.

Before you start riding, cross the street and take a spin on the **Crescent Park Carousel** (700 Bullocks Point Ave., Riverside, RI).

Go north on Bullocks Point Avenue and then right on Crescent View Avenue (Route 103A) and follow it until you see water. Turn right on . . .

The **East Bay Bike Path**. Bike approximately 5 miles to . . .

Amaral's Fish and Chips (4 Redmond St., Warren, RI).

Go south on Redmond and take the first right onto Child Street (Route 103W). Stop for a refreshing . . .

Del's Lemonade (65 Child St., Warren, RI). After Del's, continue on Child, crossing the bike path, until you get to Main Street. Turn right on Main and bike one block to Miller. Turn left on Miller to Water Street. Turn left on Water and bike about five blocks until you reach . . .

Blount Clam Shack on the Waterfront (335 Water St., Warren) on your right. After eating your cakes, turn right on Water Street until it dead ends at Bridge Street. Turn right on Bridge. In a third of a mile, turn right on the bike path. Bike 4 miles until the path ends in front of . . .

Quito's (411 Thames St., Bristol, RI).

Retrace your route back.

"ADULT" RIDE

Number of miles: 24 round-trip (31 with optional ice cream stop)

Number of clam cake joints: 6

Net calories (consumed minus expended, with ice cream stop and assuming one clam cake per stop): -250

Terrain: Mainly flat with a few tough hills over the Mount Hope Bridge and from Portsmouth to Bristol

Park: Jamiel's Park (134 Market St., Warren, RI). Take a left out of the parking lot onto Market Street and then your first right onto Redmond.

Amaral's Fish and Chips (4 Redmond St., Warren, RI) will be a half mile up on your left.

Follow directions from short ride to get to **Del's**, **Blount Clam Shack**, and **Quito's**.

Once you've finished your cakes at Quito's, turn right on Thames Street and bike along the bay (0.6 mile), turning left immediately before the dead end for one block and then right onto Route 114 (Hope Street).

Continue on 114 for 1.7 miles (with your head up—there's not much of a shoulder and quite a bit of traffic), then cross Mount Hope Bridge. Bear left after the bridge onto Boyds Lane (versus Route 138, which continues to the right). Follow Boyds about a mile until it dead ends at Park Avenue. Turn left on Park and you will soon see . . .

Flo's Drive-In (324 Park Ave., Portsmouth, RI) and **Schultzy's** (346 Park Ave., Portsmouth, RI), both on the left.

After eating clam cakes, turn left out of the parking lot and continue on that main road for several miles (bearing left onto Point and continuing as the name changes to Hummock's Point and Hummock's, taking the pedestrian overpass in the middle).

Turn right toward Common Fence Point and enter the bike lane over the big Sakonnet River Bridge (Routes 24/138). Exit right at the end of the bridge onto Central Avenue and merge right when it hits Main Road (Route 77). Follow it about a mile and a half until you see . . .

Evelyn's Drive-In (2335 Main Rd., Tiverton) on your left.

Hungry for more? Exit left out of Evelyn's and continue on Route 77 another 3.5 miles to the junction of Route 179 and an optional visit to . . .

Gray's Ice Cream (16 E Rd., Tiverton, RI).

Retrace your route back up Route 77/Central Avenue and over the Sakonnet Bridge, exiting at Anthony Road and turning right onto Boyds toward the Mount Hope Bridge and so on.

NOTE: Since both rides are loops, you might want to pace your clam cake eating and fun by splitting up the food stops in Warren (i.e., saving the Del's or Blount visits for the way back). There are a number of beaches along these routes (see p. 79) and walk-ins are free, so bring your suit and do your own mini Ironman!

THE GIFT SHOP

It all started with the plain-text bumper sticker "My other ride is a quahog," inspired by the Rhode Island state legislature designating that clam as the official "state shellfish."

"The quahog is our official state animal. Now that's pretty funny," says Asher Schofield of the Providence novelty gift store Frog & Toad.

This was 2012. At that point, Frog & Toad carried no other Rhode Island-themed products. But strong sales from locals who identify with quahoggers as much as Texans identify with cowboys—and who enjoyed confounding motorists from elsewhere with a car model they'd never heard of—changed that. Soon Frog & Toad was selling a Rhode Island pennant featuring nothing more than the state name and a sketch of that clam and a T-shirt with the same picture above the words "Quahog Country USA."

"The word is hard to understand and hard to pronounce" and so intrinsically fun "just by virtue "of having a quahog on there, Schofield argues.

The quahog "line" led to a series of local tourism posters and T-shirts, including several referring to clam-cake-selling Warwick shore resorts. "Where debris meets the sea" is the slogan on the T-shirt for the rough-scrabble Oakland Beach, home of Iggy's. The Rocky Point one merely features the state's name in the font and color of the old Rocky Point sign. (Talk about your in-jokes!)

So far the only direct reference to clam cakes in their online catalog is a drawing on their Rhode Island Foods poster. But with one Frog & Toad bag and T-shirt featuring a retro-cartoon quahog character named Clancy saying, "I'm getting stuffed" (as in a stuffie), can a Clancy clam-cake-sinker product line be far behind?

THE CARTOONIST

If (as Asher Schofield, earlier, suggests) Rhode Islanders do identify with quahogs, Don Bousquet is the man to credit or blame.

In his almost 25-year career as Rhode Island's unofficial cartoonist, Bousquet penned hundreds of quahog panels, in more than 20 best-selling books, including ones titled *I Brake for Quahogs*, *The Quahog Walks Among Us*, *The Quahog Stops Here*, *Quahog State of Mind*, *Quahogs Are a Girl's Best Friend*, and *Revenge of the Quahog*.

Despite or because of this Bousquet is one of the state's best-known and loved celebrities, the recipient of numerous honors, including a citation from the RI state legislature and a spot in the Rhode Island Heritage Hall of Fame alongside portraitist Gilbert Stuart, humorist S. J. Perlman, and Tin Pan Alley great George M. Cohan.

Bousquet didn't start out wanting to create clam comics. Like most gag cartoonists, he set his sights on the *New Yorker*. But a bunch of rejections from them coupled with the news that his wife was pregnant led him to approach local newspapers about filling the then-nonexistent role of nonpolitical Rhode Island cartoonist.

A lifetime living in the state gave him material and a short stint in the Navy stationed in California provided perspective. In a 2005 *Providence Journal* story, Bousquet recalled going to a diner in San Francisco and ordering a cabinet and a

THE HIGH PRICE OF BOBBING FOR CLAMCAKES

grinder (that is Rhode Islandese for a milkshake and Italian sub). "You want *what*?" asked the perplexed waitress. He figured out then that Rhode Islanders had a unique and funny way of doing things, a realization further honed while earning an anthropology degree at the University of Rhode Island (after getting a C in his one and only college art course).

Although his cartoons for the *Providence Journal* and *Narragansett Times* covered a whole range of Rhode Island quirks and problems (including the citizenry's inability to pronounce their Rs, need to pack a bag for any trip longer than the state's 37-mile width, and love of corrupt politicians), his clam cartoons are what produced the most reader compliments. So he started drawing more of them. So many that even he came to describe himself as "the guy who draws clams." And clam cakes.

Among Bousquet's greatest clam cake and quahog hits:

- A lawn sign next to a doghouse reading "Beware of the Quahog" with a post and chain leading into the water;
- A clammer posing beside a giant quahog in the manner of tuna fisherman above the caption "Average upper Narragansett Bay quahog taken by Mr. Rocco Cooney of Milton Ave., Cranston on Sept. 3, 1957";
- A fisherman "trolling for mermaids" with clam cake bait;
- A little kid at the dinner table complaining, "Littleneck sandwiches again?";
- Residents of the Old Quahoggers' Home with their arms still up in the air in the clam tong operator pose; and
- A cartoon of Rhode Island Civil War soldiers bearing trap-ended guns titled "Men of the 2nd R.I. Volunteers with Fixed Bullrakes, Manassas, Va., 1861."

THE BREAKFAST

Before the invention of dedicated breakfast foods, clam cakes were on at least some hotel breakfast menus.

But there's only one public place where you can still get clam cakes at 8 a.m. in Rhode Island and that's at the Oak Lawn Community Baptist Church's May Day Breakfast.

This quirky Rhode Island food tradition—one of many, you've probably figured out by now—began right here in 1867. At the time, the church needed money to build a new sanctuary, and a member came up with the idea of doing an English-style May Day celebration complete with meal and the crowning of the May queen. Seeing the Baptists get their building, other churches, granges, and social clubs copied.

Although May Breakfasts are not as common in Rhode Island as they once were, about a dozen nonprofits still hold the all-you-can-eat feasts on or around May 1 featuring the usual eggs, ham, and sausage, and sometimes also the jonnycakes and pie that were common to breakfast in pre-Froot Loops days. Most places also sell brightly decorated May Day baskets filled with candy to-go.

Oak Lawn is the only modern-day May Day Breakfast to still feature clam cakes, and if you look at the clam cake page of organizer Julie Ellison's three-inch-thick May Day Breakfast "war" manual, it's not hard to understand why.

The list of duties for setup the night before includes covering "the floor under and around fryolator with newspaper to prevent slipping." Volunteer clam cake makers are told to show up at 4:30 a.m. wearing "old clothes, shoes and long sleeves—this is a messy job!"

Why so early? Oak Lawn's first seating of 125 people is traditionally 6 a.m., and it takes at least 45 minutes to make 375 clam cakes using the church's two deep fryers (assuming an average consumption of three clam cakes per person). After that, it's pretty much non-stop clam cake making through the volunteer feeding at 11:30 a.m.

The instructions specify scooping batter by "small spoonfuls" to produce "bite size" clam cakes—a point that Ellison admits has been the subject of "a few little disagreements over the years." But "large ones take longer to cook" and "there's a certain speed of cooking you have to maintain to have a continuous supply of clam cakes."

Adds Julie's husband, May Day Breakfast co-chair Jim: "If you

Bob Kolb and Judy Butzier work the fryers at the 2022 Oak Lawn May Day Breakfast.

run out, people will sit around longer waiting for them and then the group of people who are waiting to eat have to wait longer—it's a nasty circle." The Ellisons say clam cakes are the only menu item with this potential to bring their whole carefully planned May Breakfast plan to a screeching halt.

Sounds like a menu item to consider cutting. Who wants to eat clam cakes for breakfast nowadays anyway?

"Trust me, they eat them," Julie replies, up to 320 dozen over the course of the morning.

People at an all-you-can-eat feast not being inclined to waste stomach space on something that isn't terrific, that's quite an endorsement.

THE CARNIVALS

Ask people in Maine or Southern New England for the best place to get clam cakes and you will get the name of one or more restaurants. On the Eastern Shore of Virginia, however, this same question will likely instead yield advice to go to the Wachapreague or Chincoteague volunteer firemen's carnivals.

The carnivals are a time-honored way for volunteer fire companies to raise operating expenses not covered by taxes while providing the community with good old-fashioned rides, games, and food, including clam fritters.

And guess what food was featured at fundraising dinners and drive-by takeouts held by both fire companies to help fill the fundraising gap created when both festivals were put on pause during the pandemic? It was clam fritters to the rescue again.

Chincoteague Fire Company spokeswoman Denise Bowden says that clam and oyster fritters are the most popular foods at that festival and that the lines to get one on some evenings can be as long as two hours.

The Wachapreague Carnival's fritter "cook shack"

Why all the excitement about a dish that many older local home cooks and at least a few local restaurants also still make?

"They float 'em," explains Martha Linton of Martha's Kitchen restaurant in Saxis, Virginia, meaning deep-fry them when pan-frying is the more common preparation in homes and even at Martha's. And higher-fat food always tastes better than lower.

Fundraisers like Wachapreague Fire Chief Sean Fate have their own reason for liking clam fritters. "Clams are inexpensive." In summer 2022, they were half the cost of the oysters used to make the festival's oyster fritters, and so a much better money-maker.

Fate says he's "blessed to have four women with a combined cooking experience of 300 years" frying up the Wachapreague Carnival's clam fritters, though he doesn't know exactly how they do it. "To this day Miss Berlie refuses to give me the recipe." And when Berlie Shields got sick in 2021, Miss Gracie Smith stepped up with a recipe of her own "that is also very good," and that Fate also doesn't know. "I'm not sure any of it is written down. I think it's more: Crack some eggs, a pinch of this and that, and like that."

Waterfowl hunting guide Andy Linton is Mr. Clam Fritter of Chincoteague Island and its yearly firemen's carnival. He inherited the latter post in 2006 from another volunteer fireman who was smoking on the job. In addition to making all the fritters for the carnival, he also manages the clam fritter booth at the Chincoteague Chamber's May Seafood Festival. And guess who the Museum of Chincoteague Island turned to when they wanted to put a clam fritter cooking demonstration up on their YouTube channel? That's right, Andy.

Linton actually has two clam fritter recipes: his "regulars," and his personal favorite "specials." And unlike the Wachapreague women, he shares the recipes freely. (The recipe that follows is proof.) The specials contain chopped, raw onion, Worcestershire sauce, and Old Bay in addition to the usual chopped whole chowder clams, eggs, and flour, and are too flavorful for some older people, says Linton. Officially, only "regulars" are served at the Chincoteague carnival, but it's an open secret you can get a "special" there if Linton's not too busy (rare) or if you're willing to wait.

At 76, Linton is technically also an "older" person and, after standing over a hot fryolator for six hours several days straight in the late July Virginia heat, one day four years ago suffered heat stroke and was carried out of the carnival grounds on a gurney with his apron still on.

He notes with pride how, while waiting on a cot in the hospital hallway, he overheard someone exclaim: "Hey, this is the guy who cooks clam fritters at carnival!"

He wasn't released until three days later—in other words, he nearly gave his life in the line of duty making clam fritters.

A TALE OF TWO LINTONS

Andy Linton is no near relation of Martha Linton of Martha's Kitchen, home of oversized clam fritters, though they have met. "She said we should have a cook-off. I said, 'I've dropped more fritters on the ground at carnival than you've cooked in your entire lifetime.'"

Andy Linton's Special Clam Fritters

½ gallon shucked chowder clams, with their liquor (about 17 unshucked clams and 1 cup juice)

3 eggs, beaten

1 ½ cups diced onion

1 tablespoon sugar

1 teaspoon salt

1 tablespoon pepper

3 tablespoons Old Bay seasoning

2 teaspoons Worcestershire sauce

2 cups flour (more or less, as necessary)

Vegetable oil for frying

Preheat oil in a deep fryer or a cast iron pan (in this case, with 1 to 2 inches of oil) to 360°F. Mix clams with liquor, eggs, onion, sugar, salt, pepper, seasoning, and Worcestershire, and 1 cup flour and keep adding flour until you have something resembling a thick muffin batter.

Carefully lay ⅓ to ½ cup of batter onto oil with a round ladle. (If temperature is right, batter should bubble.) Fry until edge is golden and the middle puffs up slightly, about 7 minutes, then turn and fry the other side an additional 3 minutes or until both sides are golden brown. Drain well on paper towels. Serve on hamburger buns or on a platter with sides.

Yield: About 15 burger-sized fritters

COME FOR THE FRITTERS AND STAY FOR THE PONIES

Although the deep-fried clam fritters are reason enough for people who bought this book to go to Chincoteague in July, there is something else going on there that month that you might want to know about. We are talking, of course, about ponies.

Chincoteague and nearby Assateague Islands have been home to a bunch of wild ponies—technically, actually little horses—since the 1700s. However the ponies got there—some say they survived a Spanish shipwreck, others that colonists hid them there to avoid English taxes—the annual wild-animal roundup or pony penning was a locals-only thing until Marguerite Henry visited the island during penning week in the 1940s and wrote *Misty of Chincoteague*. The story of a brother and sister and two of these ponies has captured the hearts of children before and since. (The 1947 book is still in print.)

The result: Chincoteague now has a Pony Express tourist trolley, a Pony Tails Candy Shop, Sandy Pony Donuts, a Purple Pony T-shirt shop, and Salt-water Pony Boat Tours cashing in on the 30 to 40 thousand people who swarm the island's 37 square miles the last week of July. They are there to witness the pony's annual swim from Assateague to Chincoteague and the subsequent fundraising and herd-trimming auction of some of the herd's foals.

The actual swim, which takes place on Wednesday morning, is considered the highlight but is the most crowded and requires getting up early in the morning and waiting hours in a muddy marsh or rented boat for something that lasts all of five minutes.

Fortunately, there are many other opportunities to see the ponies up close that week that are not as fraught. For instance, the pony round-up before the swim and the parade to the fairgrounds for clam fritters after. (That last part about the fritters is a joke: As locals, the ponies know to get their fritters

The northern island–situated pony herd meets the southern during Chincoteague penning week's beach walk.

earlier in the month, when lines are shorter.) There are also free daily show-ings of the *Misty* movie at the island's theater. (Before you go in, look down at the sidewalk adorned Grauman Theatre-style with Misty's footprints.)

Although Misty and her foal Stormy (star of an also-famous book sequel) are both long gone, their taxidermized remains are a major draw of the Museum of Chincoteague Island year-round.

THE OTHER FUNDRAISERS

Chincoteague and Wachapreague Volunteer Firemen's carnivals may be the largest fundraisers featuring clam fritters, but they're far from the only ones. Here's a taste of some others.

The **clam fritter luncheon** held at the beginning of every year at the **Remson United Methodist Church** in Pocomoke City, Maryland (about 20 miles northwest of Chincoteague), has its roots in a raccoon and ham dinner the church held many years ago. "Then rabies developed in the coon population around here, and we switched to chicken and dumplings," and later, clam frit-ters, says church member Jennifer Porter. The luncheon includes the fritters, hot dogs (for people who don't like fritters), and peas and dumplings (a not-so-well-known Southern soup).

The luncheon is an eagerly anticipated church and community event. In fact, Porter says, the only complaint they've ever gotten is about the size of the fritter rolls. "People say, 'What's with the miniature rolls?'" The rolls are actually standard hamburger buns, but the fritters are so big, they hang over.

Porter said the most memorable fritter luncheon occurred seven or eight years ago on the day a big snowstorm was predicted. "It was sunny in the morning, but by the time we finished, it was a blizzard. We still had it, and people still waited in line—in fact, we sold out," she said.

Clams for the Remson Church luncheon—and most of the other small clam fritter fundraisers on the Eastern Shore—are harvested by organization members. But bad weather and elusive clams in 2022 caused the **Men's Club of Johnson's United Methodist Church** in Machipongo, Virginia, to postpone their **annual spring clam fritter dinner** for the first time ever. Originally sched-uled for April 29, the date was changed to a month later and then to "when-ever we get enough clams." (By early July, the men had 1,800 clams shucked, ground, and frozen but still needed 600 more.) In bi-monthly updates on their clam-catching progress, club member Kenneth Webb was both apologetic and concerned. "The clams just don't seem to be there anymore, and nobody knows why." The dinner dates back to at least the 1950s and typically attracts up to 200 combined locals and ex-locals—doubling as an "old home week"-like event for those who've moved away.

How popular are clam cakes in Rhode Island? So popular that even Polish festivals serve them. Louise Pankiewicz-DiCarlo of **Our Lady of Czenstochowa's**

Ted Drozdz welcomes non-Polish food lovers at Our Lady of Czenstochowa's summer festival.

Roman Catholic Parish in Coventry, Rhode Island, says clam cakes and chowder were added to the half-century-old **summer Polish festival** back when Catholics were prohibited from eating meat on Fridays. They were a meat-fast friendly alternative to the festival's homemade pierogies, golombki, and kapusta. Now the clam cakes are also served on Saturdays "until our batter runs out." Most memorable in the annals of Czenstochowa clam cake making was the year of "the batter explosion—the batter was put in a refrigerator that wasn't holding its temperature" and the baking powder in the mix did its thing. This festival is also famous for cow chip bingo. Explains Pankiewicz-DiCarlo: "It's a gridded space where folks take a chance. The cow . . . does a little walk around and hopefully leaves a deposit on someone's square."

Clam cakes have long been a loss leader for the **Warren (RI) Rotary Club's** annual **Quahog Festival**. Prior to each year's festival, traditionally held in July, the club would distribute coupons for six free clam cakes with any other festival food purchase. To keep up with the demand that created, club members modified a doughnut machine to spit out 24 inch-and-a-quarter clam cakes a minute. Next up for these Warren Rotary geniuses: the world's first perpetual motion machine.

CLAM CAKE/FRITTER CALENDAR OF EVENTS

March: RI Quahog Week, special clam-focused menus and events, various locations in RI, dem.ri.gov.

First Saturday in May: Chincoteague Seafood Festival, Chincoteague, VA, chincoteague.com.

Late May: Newport Oyster and Chowder Festival, Newport, RI, Saturday and Sunday, bowenswharf.com.

Mid-June to July 4 weekend: Wachapreague Volunteer Firemen's Carnival, Wachapreague, VA, Wednesday through Saturday evenings, wachapreague.info.

July: Chincoteague Volunteer Firemen's Carnival, Chincoteague, VA. Friday and Saturday evenings in July plus Monday through Saturday the last week, chincoteague.com.

Third weekend in July: Yarmouth Clam Festival, Yarmouth, ME, clamfestival .com, and Warren Quahog Festival, Warren, RI, eastbaychamberri.org.

First weekend in August: Charlestown Seafood Festival, Charlestown, RI, charlestownseafoodfestival.com.

Second weekend in September: RI Seafood Festival, Providence, RI, rise afoodfest.com.

Early October: Chincoteague Oyster Festival, Chincoteague, VA, chincoteague .com.

Mid-October: Essex ClamFest, Essex, MA, Saturday, capeannchamber.com. (See Essex Firehouse Clam Fritter recipe that follows.)

Mid-October: Bowen's Wharf Seafood Festival, Newport, RI, Saturday and Sunday, bowenswharf.com.

Essex Firehouse Clam Fritters

This is the recipe the Essex (Massachusetts) firemen used to make RI-style clam fritters for their town's annual fall ClamFest for many years. Longtime firefighter Richard Dort says the firemen got this all-Jiffy brand recipe from a local Roman Catholic church that used to use it for its fundraising clam cake and chowder dinners.

  1 (40-ounce) box Jiffy Baking Mix

  1 (8.5-ounce) box Jiffy Corn Muffin Mix

  1 teaspoon salt

  4 teaspoons baking powder

  4 eggs

  4 cups clam juice

  4 cups chopped clams

Blend Jiffy mixes with salt and baking powder in a very large bowl. In a separate bowl, beat eggs into clam juice; then add clams. Slowly combine wet and dry ingredients. Let batter sit overnight in the refrigerator. Heat frying oil to 350°F. Drop half a standard ice cream scoop of batter into the oil and cook until golden brown—about 4 minutes.

Yield: 70 to 90 fritters or enough for 2 to 3 dozen people

4
DIY CLAM CAKES AND FRITTERS

Clam fritters are beach and festival fare. Next to those fun-time associations, one of the best things about them is that other people do the messy job of frying them up for you.

But what if you're nowhere near where you can buy a fritter? That's where this chapter comes in. Use it to conjure up summertime coastal clam deliciousness anytime and place. Frying fritters might be messy, but it isn't difficult. If you can make pancakes, you can make clam cakes!

Rhode Island Clam Cakes (Balls): The Basic Standard

This recipe offers time-tested proportions of wet to dry ingredients but also options as to what those wet and dry ingredients should be.

The main dry ingredient in most Southern New England clam cakes is flour; the few that also include cornmeal don't use very much. Using majority cornmeal will push your clam cakes dangerously close to Southern hush puppy territory (and will also require cutting back on the liquid in the recipe by a quarter to a half).

As for the clams: The minimum amount specified should ensure at least a few in every clam cake. Although no one will complain if you add more, clam flavor is what you're really after, and that can come just as easily and more cheaply by making your liquid all clam broth or at least using it half-and-half with milk.

    2 cups of all-purpose flour (or cornmeal or some combination)

    ½ teaspoon salt (or more, to taste)

    ⅛ teaspoon pepper

    2 teaspoons baking powder

    1 tablespoon sugar (optional)

    2 eggs

    1 cup milk or clam juice or some combination

    2 tablespoons butter, melted or oil (optional)

    1 (or more) cups chopped or minced clams

    Oil for frying (canola, peanut, melted shortening or even lard)

Combine the flour and/or cornmeal, salt, pepper, powder, and sugar (if using) in a large bowl. In a small bowl, beat the eggs then blend with the milk and/or clam juice and butter (if using). Gently fold wet ingredients into dry, then stir in clams. Batter should be the consistency of thick muffin batter; if not, adjust with more liquid or flour.

Pour about 2 inches of oil in a deep fryer, Dutch oven, or large frying pan and heat to 360 to 375°F. (One test, if you don't have a fryer thermometer: A cube of bread dropped into the oil should brown in no more than a minute.) Drop batter by teaspoon-, tablespoon-, or ice cream scoop-full into the hot oil—the balls should sink, then rise and float. Fry, turning once, in about 5 minutes, when the underside is golden brown.

Continue cooking until the other side is also brown, an additional 3 or 4 minutes. Remove with a slotted spoon and drain on a paper towel. It's a good idea to taste your first cake so that you can adjust the seasoning, if needed. Thereafter, fry as many cakes as will fit without crowding.

Yield: About 2 dozen medium-sized clam balls or enough to serve 6 to 8 as an appetizer

Maine Clam Cakes (Patties): The Basic Standard

The simplicity of this recipe is a consequence of its age and how infrequently Maine residents make clam cakes at home these days. And fans of old-fashioned New England cooking think that simplicity is a good thing (at least for the integrity of this dish, which is usually deep-fried at restaurants but pan-fried at home, as it is here).

These were traditionally made with pilot crackers. Vermont Common is one brand that's still available. Otherwise use saltines, oyster crackers, or, for a richer taste, Ritz.

2 cups chopped clams

1 ½ cups cracker crumbs

2 eggs

¼ teaspoon salt (only if using pilot or other unsalted crackers)

¼ cup clam juice (optional)

3 to 4 tablespoons butter, for frying

Mix clams with 1 ¼ cups of the cracker crumbs in a bowl. Stir in the eggs, one at a time, and salt, if using, then let the mixture sit until the crumbs are moist and the mixture holds together, at least 15 minutes. Add clam juice if it seems too dry. Mold the mixture into four patties about ½-inch thick. Spread remaining crumbs out evenly on a flat surface. Press both sides of the patties on the crumbs.

Place butter in a frying pan under medium heat until melted and bubbling. Put the patties in the pan and fry until brown on one side, then turn and brown on the other. Serve as an appetizer or side dish or as a "clamburger"—in a hamburger bun.

Yield: 4 servings

Eastern Shore Clam Fritters (Pancakes): The Basic Standard

Clam fritters are more of a home than a restaurant dish in rural coastal Maryland and Virginia, and so there are almost as many ways to make them as home chefs. But this is a basic, starter recipe.

Many people also add onion, and a few add paprika or Old Bay seasoning. See p. 136 for one of these gussied-up, deep-fried versions popular at local summer carnivals.

2 cups minced clams, drained

2 eggs, beaten

1 teaspoon baking powder

½ teaspoon salt

¼ teaspoon pepper

½ cup of clam juice or milk or some combination

½ to 1 ½ cup all-purpose flour

¼ cup vegetable oil

Combine clams and eggs in a bowl. Add baking powder, salt, and pepper. Add ½ cup liquid and ½ cup flour and continue adding flour by ¼ cups until the batter holds together. (You don't want the cakes to taste more of flour than clam!) Batter should be the consistency of thick pancake batter or slightly thicker.

Pour the oil in a medium-sized skillet on medium heat until it is hot. Drop three ⅛-cup-mounds of the batter into the pan like you would pancakes, and, if necessary, pat them down with a spoon or spatula so they're about 6 inches around and ½- to ¾-inch thick.

Turn the heat down to medium-low and cook until the top looks dry and the bottom is browned, about 5 minutes. Then flip and cook the other side for another 5 to 7 minutes.

Remove from heat and serve on hamburger buns or on a plate with potato chips, baked beans, or potato salad. These also can be made silver-dollar-sized and served as an appetizer.

Yield: 8 fritters

NOTE: Bisquick or Pearl Milling (formerly Aunt Jemima) is sometimes used in place of the flour: If you want to do that, omit or cut back on the baking powder.

GILDING THE CLAM CAKE

Food that eats classic and pure to a New Englander can seem bland to people from elsewhere, especially if those people went to culinary school. That explains all the newfangled ingredients that are starting to show up in clam fritters and clam fritter recipes. (Here's looking at you Dune Brothers and Sam Sifton.)

Here are some of the most common ingredients chefs are adding to their clam cake batter (listed in rough order of popularity) that you might want to try also. Note: All solid ingredients should be finely chopped.

Beer or buttermilk (in place of some or all of the liquid), onion (or scallions or shallots or chive), garlic, bell pepper, ground paprika, thyme, fresh parsley, jalapeno or other hot pepper, Tabasco, sriracha, hot pepper flakes, cayenne powder or Old Bay, celery, brown sugar or maple syrup (in place of the optional sugar in our basic recipe), and chourico or linguica sausage.

Those last two are a popular clam cake addition at seafood eateries in the Portuguese-influenced New Bedford/Fall River area of Massachusetts. To prevent the clam flavor from being overwhelmed, keep your sausage-to-clam ratio around one-to-three or at the most one-to-two.

Actually, you shouldn't use too much of *any* of these additions (How much is too much? More than a teaspoon of the powders or sauces) or a small amount of too many all at once: That will turn this just-folks food into spicy Caribbean conch territory.

SPECIAL SAUCE

Worried about ruining your fritters with one of these new-fangled additions? A compromise position involves pairing traditional clam fritters with a flavorful tartar or non-traditional spicy sauce that are all the rage with some newer clam cake places.

The flavor will be improved in those sauces that contain mayonnaise if you make your own and, in all cases, if the ingredients have a chance to meld together in the refrigerator for a few hours before serving.

Basic Traditional Tartar

Because I believe in using what you already have rather than buying a bunch of specialty sauces (like tartar, especially if you eat fried seafood at home infrequently).

½ cup mayonnaise

2 tablespoons sweet pickle relish

1 tablespoon lemon juice

1 ½ tablespoons onion, finely chopped

Maine Tartar

Dill pickles are a traditional accompaniment to Maine clam cakes, and Ken's Place in Saco also serves a very dill-pickle-heavy tartar. This is my attempt to reproduce it.

¾ cup mayonnaise

½ cup finely chopped dill pickle, liquid drained and reserved

2 tablespoons dill pickle juice

1 tablespoon lemon juice

1 tablespoon onion, finely chopped

Gochujang Tartar

Damon Todd of Portland Lobster Company in Portland, Maine, serves this spicy sauce alongside his house-made clam cakes.

2 cups mayonnaise

3 tablespoons cornichons, diced

3 tablespoons capers, chopped roughly

2 teaspoons pickling liquid from the cornichons

⅛ cup of gochujang (Korean fermented chili paste)

½ teaspoon salt

Chipotle Mayo

1 cup mayonnaise

2 tablespoons canned chipotle peppers in adobo, minced

2 tablespoons lemon or lime juice

1 ½ teaspoons garlic, minced

3 tablespoons fresh cilantro, finely chopped

Spicy Remoulade

¾ cup mayonnaise

3 tablespoons mustard

1 tablespoon horseradish

1 tablespoon sweet paprika

1 teaspoon hot sauce or to taste

1 ½ teaspoons Creole or Cajun seasoning

1 teaspoon lemon juice

1 clove garlic, minced

Spicy Mayo Ketchup

4 tablespoons mayonnaise

3 tablespoons ketchup

1 tablespoon hot sauce

1 tablespoon lime juice

HISTORICAL HELP

"Will some reader give me the recipe for clam cakes like the ones you get at shore dinners along the Providence River?" asked E. L. of Franklin, Massachusetts, in the recipe swap column of March 11, 1895's *Boston Globe*.

Two days later, Mrs. C. J. D. of Roxbury, responded with "1 pint of sifted flour, ⅔ teaspoon of baking powder, a little pepper and salt; mix thoroughly with 1 egg and just enough milk to take up all the dry flour; drain 1 pint of clams and chop fine; stir into the batter, drop into hot lard from small greased spoon."

How much milk should that be exactly?

Like most of the many recipes for clam fritters that were published in newspapers and cookbooks at the turn-of-the-nineteenth-century height of its shore dinner popularity, this one is unhelpfully vague. The modern cook might also be frustrated by strange words like gill as in "a gill of milk" (about half a cup), saleratus (an archaic term for baking soda), and spyder (a frying pan with spider-like legs, so that it could sit over an open fire).

But these old recipes also offer some ideas that seem new and possibly worth considering—like dipping your spoon in the grease before dipping it into a sticky dough, as in the recipe above. The frequent use of sour milk in place of what was then called "sweet" milk in other old recipes could lend tang and greater lightness to modern clam cakes.

In ingredients and proportions, the fritter recipe in the 1904 edition of *The Home Science Cook Book*, by Mary J. Lincoln and Anna Barrows, is virtually identical to our basic, standard RI one except for Lincoln and Barrows's suggested possible one additional teaspoon of baking powder and one tablespoon of lemon juice or vinegar, and the suggested possible omission of one egg, or the yolks of both eggs.

Whatever your decision on the eggs, the recipe gives intriguing non-optional instructions to separate the yolks and whites, whip the whites until stiff and fold them into the batter at the very end. It's an extra step that contemporary clam fritter recipe writers Sam Sifton and Jasper White both also advocate.

CLAM FRITTERS FOR SPECIAL DIETS

Clam cakes traditionally contain clams, flour, and milk or milk byproducts, and so most restaurant ones will be off-limits for vegans, celiacs, and the lactose intolerant. But it's not that hard to make clam fritters that accommodate these special diets.

Celiacs can use A & J Bakery's Gluten Free Clam Cake Mix (see p. 149) or make their own gluten-free cakes by swapping out commercially available gluten-free flour or baking mix for the regular kind in recipes. (Bob's Red Mill is one brand that makes both products.) Olive oil and clam juice or beer can seamlessly stand in for butter and milk, respectively, in standard clam fritter recipes for the lactose intolerant.

Making vegan clam cakes is more of a challenge. The often-derided scarcity of clams in Rhode Island-style fritters helps here. Oyster mushrooms cut up in chunks and "clam juice" made with dulce flakes, nori seaweed sheets or kelp powder, and warm water are the substitutes of choice for most vegan Internet bloggers. Vegans and vegetarians trying to recreate the almost all-clam patty fritters of Virginia and Maine might be better off making mushroom or eggplant fritters.

IN THE UNLIKELY EVENT YOU FIND YOURSELF WITH SOME EXTRA CLAM FRITTERS

Overeating is the usual solution. Should you have the self-discipline to instead store them away and save them for a hungry day, the air fryer is the best way to bring them back to life, says Julie Ellison of the Oak Lawn Community Baptist Church in Cranston, Rhode Island, who often finds herself with leftover clam cakes from her church's annual May Day Breakfast. Microwaving can leave them soggy, and reheating in the regular oven brings out the grease, but with air frying, "It's like they just came out of the fryolator," she says. Ellison recommends preheating the air fryer to 350°F, then cooking for five minutes, shaking the pan, then cooking for five minutes more. Note that we're only talking about reheating here. This popular appliance isn't anyone's first choice for making wet batter food like clam cakes.

THE MIX MATCH

Don't want to bother making Rhode Island-style clam cakes from scratch? There's a mix for that.

In fact, many restaurants and clam shacks today use mixes to make clam cakes quickly and consistently. So, if your goal is to recreate the taste of a clam cake from one of those places, using the mix they use might be the best way to go.

The most popular mix with restaurants by far is Drum Rock, though Krisppe, Kenyon's, and even the old standby Bisquick also have their fans.

The Aunt Carrie's and Iggy's mixes are more recent entries targeted to home cooks.

Most of these mixes contain flour, leavener (usually baking powder), and whey (milk). All require clams and clam juice in addition to the mix but most of these products' instructions lump these two ingredients together in a way that can be problematic.

Four ounces of clams and clam juice could mean 1 ounce of chopped clam meat and 3 ounces of clam juice, or 3 ounces of chopped clam meat and 1 ounce of clam juice, but the former will create quite a different batter than the latter. When in doubt, add liquids to these mixes last and in stages until you have something resembling a thick muffin batter.

Also, though most specify a 350°F or lower frying temperature, that was too low for the little deep fryer I was using, producing cakes that were too greasy from a too-long time in the oil. If you have that problem, try raising the temperature 10°F or 15°F.

On the plus side: None of these mixes produced the dreaded sinkers.

Here are some additional notes from my mix taste-test. (Mixes are listed in impartial alphabetical order.)

A & J Bakeries Gluten Free Clam Cake Mix. $8.49 per two-pound bag at the bakery (1458 Park Ave., Cranston, RI), select Dave's Fresh Marketplaces or via aandjbakery.net.

Joe Hitzemann—the J of A&J nut- and gluten-free bakery—first developed this gluten- and dairy-free clam cake mix almost 12 years ago for Robert Bedrick, the owner of Krisppe regular clam cake mix (described further in this section) before Hitzemann bought that retail business from him. I've got to assume the instructions on his gluten-free package now are much newer because it's hard to imagine anyone buying this mix more than once after following them. The called-for half cup of clam juice barely dampens two pounds of this corn-and-rice-flour blend, never mind creating a batter wet enough to drop. Two times the juice makes heavy fritters; four times is more like it.

The good news is once you figure that out, these fry up quite nicely: The insides are more uniform than ones made with flour and the flavor a bit blander but that could easily be remedied with a few flavor add-ins (see p. 144 for some suggestions). And the all-important crust is light and crunchy.

In fact, this is probably the best gluten-free "baked good" I've ever eaten.

The Original Aunt Carrie's Clam Cake and Fritter Mix. $7 to $9 per 1.5-pound bag at the restaurant, Dave's Fresh Marketplaces, or through auntcarriesri.com. The largest package of the conventional-flour mixes and the only one with a resealable bag (though it only offers instructions for one-time use). Aunt Carrie's is also the only mix besides Bisquick to call for eggs. Surprisingly, this did not make the finished cakes taste appreciably richer than Drum Rock or Iggy's, which they resembled in mainstream clam cake acceptability. In short, good but not as good as Aunt Carrie's (possibly because the restaurant uses lard and has a hundred years more experience at this than I do).

Bisquick Pancake & Baking Mix. $2.50 and up per 20-ounce box at supermarkets everywhere. Yes, you can make clam cakes with Bisquick. Just add two cups of the mix, a half cup of milk or clam juice (or some combination), and another half cup of clams. Bisquick clam cakes were crispier than any other mix-made cakes not containing corn—perhaps because of the vegetable oil Bisquick—and only Bisquick—contains. They were also quite salty.

Drum Rock Products Fritter and Clam Cake Mix. $4.99 and up per one-pound bag at famousfoods.com and some seafood markets (see drumrockproducts.com for a list). This mix suffered most from not specifying a clam-to-juice ratio, producing a batter that was unusably thin. But when remade with less liquid, these cakes were—surprise, surprise!—reminiscent of ones served by stands who use Drum Rock. That is, they were crispy on the outside and doughy in. That's probably why this mix is so popular with restaurants. (Certainly no one is attracted by their industrial-looking plain-white-sack packaging.) See p. 61 for more on the Drum Rock company.

Iggy's Fritter & Clam Cake Mix. $5 and up per one-pound box at the restaurants, Dave's Fresh Marketplaces, or iggysri.com and goldbelly.com. One of three mixes that tells you to let the batter sit before frying. Krisppe and Iggy's batter both rise like bread dough during that time. The results here are good if a bit plain, which is also how some describe Iggy's stand cakes.

Kenyon's Clam Cake and Fritter Mix. $6.99 and up per one-pound box at some fish markets, famousfoods.com, their store, or via kenyonsgristmill.com. One of few mixes containing corn—in this case, stoneground cornmeal from a storied Rhode Island gristmill depicted on this mix's beautifully retro box. That box also guilelessly (stupidly?) boasts that the mix "will last indefinitely in your refrigerator." (See pp. 150–152 for Kenyon's back story, including its recent financial woes.) The cakes this makes have a big crunch and a fine interior crumb that melts in your mouth when hot like an excellent hush puppy.

Krisppe Clam Cake Seasoned Batter Mix. $3 and up per 10-ounce bag at some seafood markets, Dave's Fresh Marketplaces, and amazon.com. Another mix containing corn and the only mix that specified the amount of clams and clam juice needed in its (to me, welcome) fussy directions. It produced a bread-dough-like batter and a crispy cake with a flavorful interior, perhaps because of the paprika and rosemary former longtime owner Robert Bedrick says are part of the recipe along with corn. Krisppe is also the only one of these mixes to contain egg. Whatever the reason, this produced my favorite cakes of this testing.

Kenyon's: A Clam Cake Tradition Grinds On

Drum Rock's status as clam-cake-mix king of Southern New England is largely a secret. That's because Drum Rock mainly sells its fritter mix to restaurants that would rather keep their use of a mix or any other pre-prepared item on the QT.

If Rhode Islanders know any clam cake mix at all, it is Kenyon's.

The company stoked its fame by selling clam cakes at fairs and festivals and by giving tours of its historic gristmill, a clapboard building by a waterfall on the Queen's River so quaint that it would be worth visiting even if the company didn't give tours and rent out kayaks.

They're also known just from being around so long—since 1696. Kenyon's is, in fact, the oldest manufacturing business and the second-oldest business of any kind in Rhode Island.

The mill in this tiny village of Usquepaug—the "new building"— was built in 1886, after the 1696 one burnt down. The Kenyons lent their name in 1909. Computer repairman Paul Drumm Jr. bought the business in 1971 with the idea of turning it into a craft shop for his

The gristmill home of Kenyon's Clam Cake and Fritter Mix is quaint incarnate.

wife. But history won out, and under the tutelage of Narragansett Indian Charles Walmsley, Drumm became a miller.

The grains are ground between two big, stacked wheels of rough-textured granite, explained Paul Drumm III, during a recent walkthrough. Paul inherited the business from his dad and now works it with his son, Ben.

Kernels are fed into the stationary stone, then crushed by the spinning top wheel. The distance between the two stones determines the fineness of the meal and can be adjusted by the miller. Walmsley could tell if the grind was right from the sound of the stones alone, Paul says admiringly.

Kenyon's sells the resulting flours and grains by themselves but also combined with other ingredients in mixes to make pancakes, corn and brown bread, jonnycakes (RI corn pancakes), and clam cakes, their best-seller. The term is relative.

Paul has been open about his struggles to make what is essentially a living history museum into a profitable business. But those struggles came to a head in 2019, when after 60 years at the Eastern States Exposition—New England's largest fair—Kenyon's lost its booth. "No, no, no!" said one fan on Facebook at the news. "State of Rhode Island, stop the insanity," posted another.

Exposition management said Kenyon's was arrears on payments, which Paul concedes. "But how can I pay that off when they're cutting off the source of almost 40 percent of my annual sales?" says Paul, the emotion rising in his voice three years after the fact. "And then to have them give that booth—in the *Rhode Island* Building—to a *Massachusetts* company," he sputters, referring to Blount, a long-time Warren, Rhode Island, seafood processor and soup maker that moved its headquarters to Fall River, Massachusetts, in 2004. This is followed by a 20-minute rant/monologue on how Paul thinks Blount got the Big E spot (Cliff Notes version: politics) and how he thinks Blount is doing there (not well).

Paul on the Big E is like a veteran on his time in combat. Stressful as those two weeks of long lines of clam cake seekers were, they were also exciting and a highlight of his year, if not his life. The termination has left him suffering a kind of PBESD (Post Big E Stress Disorder).

Kenyon's held its last annual fall Johnny Cake Festival in 2013 and is now frying up clam cakes at only two festivals in nearby Charlestown: the Seafood Festival and Rhythm & Roots. At the 2021 Seafood one, Ben Drumm coaxed golden golf-balls out of an antique dropper designed by his grandfather in the back of the Kenyon's booth while his brother, John, filled little waxed paper bags to overflowing with hot orbs at the front counter.

They're much smaller and lighter than the Drum Rocks being sold by Boy Scouts across the fairground aisle and have a pillowy texture. Ben credits the cornmeal in their recipe that's not in Drum Rock or many other clam cakes. Though not that easy to taste, "The corn keeps them from absorbing so much grease," he explains.

If you can't make these festivals, you can make your own Kenyon's clam cakes using their mix, which is sold in their gift shop. The shop is open most weekends for sales and tours (really more a chance to talk to Paul or Ben and see the grindstones and packaging area—they don't mill on weekends). They're scheduled for 1 p.m. both days, but when a family showed up in Usquepaug at 9 p.m. on a Thursday desperate to check off "U" on their quest to visit everyplace in Rhode Island A to Zed, Paul showed them around by flashlight.

Yes, Kenyon's is that kind of charming little business.

Clams: A Buying Guide

A home cook interested in making their own clam fritters has several options for procuring the dish's namesake ingredient.

The most obvious and convenient way to buy clams is in cans. They are readily available at supermarkets across the country in a 6.5-ounce size that yields about a third of a cup of chopped or minced cooked clams and a half cup of juice. These are usually cooked sea clams, or the same type of clam many clam stands use—though theirs are usually fresh.

Clam juice is also important to a cake's clam flavor, and bottled juice is generally considered superior to the juice that comes in the cans. You can find eight-ounce bottles of it next to the canned clams.

Some supermarkets and fish markets also sell (slightly less processed) frozen cooked clams (a 10.6-ounce package of Pane Pesca brand contains one and a half cups of meat and a quarter cup of juice).

At fish markets in Southern Rhode Island, Portland, Maine, and on the Eastern Shore of Virginia, home cooks can also buy the same fresh-shucked minced sea clams used by most restaurants by the pound at the seafood counter—and sometimes fresh or frozen shucked quahog as well. But outside of clam fritter land, the most you can hope for is the chance to buy all sizes of hard-shell clams—including quahogs—in the shell by the bag, pound, or individual clam.

Fish market clams are likely to be fresher than ones from a super-market. How to tell? The shells of fresh ones will be tightly closed and grey- or black-colored versus white-ish.

Shoreline residents who don't mind sloshing around in the mud and muck can ensure clam freshness by digging their own. This is standard for many families and nonprofits who hold clam fritter fund-raisers on the Eastern Shore of Virginia. How and where to do that in Virginia and the other areas discussed in this book is a book in itself!

However acquired, clams in their shells require shucking, which, if you're new at it, could get you to an emergency room faster than attempting to slice a bagel for the first time. Shucking is a breeze if you steam or bake the clams first, but that can toughen them. One end-around recommended by Virginia clam fritter chef Andy Tyler and others is to put the shelled clams into the freezer for two to three hours. Then you should be able to open them with a butter knife—over a bowl, to catch all the precious juice—before hand-chopping, scissor-cutting, or mincing the clams in a meat grinder or food processor. (Eight chowder clams should yield about a cup of shucked meat and a third of a cup of juice; the same number of cherrystones, perhaps half that.)

All of which might lead the work-averse to wonder: How impor-tant are fresh clams in a dish that—in its Rhode Island rendition, at least—is, at most, 90 percent fried dough to 10 percent clam?

Famed New England seafood chef Jasper White says using fresh clams is very important and using fresh clam juice over canned or bot-tled even more so. "A two-year-old could tell the difference," he argues.

I don't know about a two-year-old. But when this much older per-son did a side-by-side comparison of clam cakes made with canned clams and ones made with fresh surf clams, there was no compari-son: The fresh clam cakes not only tasted more like clam, they were moister and smelled sweet in the way of fresh fish. The canned clam ones were only vaguely seafoody, as reminiscent of canned tuna as of clam.

CLAM-CAKE-MAKING TIPS FROM THE MASTERS

For Southern New England-style clam cakes:

- Clams and clam juice can be salty, so be conservative about adding salt to the batter until you've tasted a sample cake. For similar reasons, Drum Rock Products president Stephen Hinger doesn't recommend using clam juice for any more than half the batter liquid.

- Want your clams to be in the dough versus the crust? Mix them into the dry ingredients before adding any liquid so that the clams get coated in flour, as per Rick Browne's game-changing suggestion (explained on p. 58).

- Don't overmix. It's the primary cause of those dreaded clam cake "sinkers," says Hinger. He says any batter with baking powder in it should instead be folded together gently.

- The ideal consistency for a Rhode Island clam cake has been variously described as like peanut butter or thick waffle or muffin batter. It should not run off the spoon but instead take a few seconds—or the helpful push of a second spoon—to lazily drop into the fat.

- Let the batter sit at least an hour in the fridge—ideally more like three to five hours—before making the fritters, says legendary New England seafood chef Jasper White. This allows time for the flavors to meld and the baking powder to do its work. (But get the batter back close to room temp before you begin cooking.)

- Leave the baseball-sized clam cakes to the pros at Aunt Carrie's and Evelyn's. Home chefs are safer making theirs small—say ping-pong-ball or even silver-dollar size, says Paul Drumm III of Kenyon's Grist Mill. Small clam cakes will cook quickly inside and out; giant ones can burn on the outside and still not be completely cooked in the middle.

For Eastern Shore-style clam fritters:

- Flour content is critical: Too little and you won't be able to flip the fritter. Too much and the fritter won't crisp up properly, several amateur fritter makers advised author Bernard Herman for his book, *A South You Never Ate.*

- Use a ladle rather than a spoon to drop your batter, says Chincoteague clam fritter king Andy Linton. A spoon will leave a triangle on one side that will cook faster than the rest of the fritter; a ladle will create the round cake you want.

For all deep-fried clam fritters:

- Make sure the oil is the right temperature (usually 350°F to 375°F) before you start cooking, and don't overload your pan or fryer with food. If you do, the temperature will drop, and your clam cakes will absorb too much grease.

- If and ONLY if you can do it safely (i.e., without using a long extension cord, and not in the middle of a storm or near kids playing ball), clam cakes are a great outdoor barbecue treat. Even if you're not near the water, it conjures up the atmosphere of the amusement parks and festivals where this food has long been enjoyed. This will also keep the mess and smell of frying out of the house.

- To prevent splashing, lay the batter on the oil close to the surface versus dropping from on high, Andy Linton advises.

- Keep your oil clean by fishing any stray pieces of batter or crumbs out of the oil with a slotted spoon as you fry and definitely before they burn or discolor the oil, advised food writer James Villas in *Southern Fried*.

- A lot of people recommend placing just-cooked clam cakes on paper towels to absorb extra grease. But this can make their crispy outsides soggy. To avoid this, chef Jacques Pepin puts them on a wire cooling rack over brown paper.

- Don't reuse oil more than a few times and only after filtering and safely storing in the refrigerator. (After the oil is completely cool, put a coffee filter in a funnel and strain the oil back into its original container.) Even when still safe, old oil can lose its crisping abilities and add off-flavors, says Jasper White.

- As for product recommendations: Everyone loves lard—even chefs who don't use it because of health concerns. Ye Olde English Fish & Chips compromises by using a lard-vegetable blend. Clabber Girl is the game-changing favorite baking powder to Jack Piemonte Jr. of Cap'n Jack's. And the secret to the wonderful texture of the cakes at N.O. Bar Clam Shack in Charlestown, Rhode Island, according to chef Saleem Nassir? Pillsbury Best All Purpose Flour, living up to its name.

THE CLAM CAKE ARTIST

Want to create a clam cake zoo or Rorschach test?—that is, a Rhode Island-style clam cake with lots of fried appendages: Use a spoon to drop the batter, instead of an ice cream scoop. And drop the batter slowly while moving the spoon slightly versus quickly and efficiently.

Restaurant Index

Recipe Index

Text and Photo Credits

Text and photos by Carolyn Wyman except for the following photographs (or specified illustrations, recipes, or text) not elsewhere credited, for which grateful acknowledgment is made:

p. xi: photo by John H. White (U.S. National Archives @ Flickr Commons); pp. 2–4: Providence Public Library; p. 6: inuyaki.com @ Flickr Commons; pp. 7 and 9: Warwick (R.I.) Historical Society; p. 13: Ed Serowik Sr.; p. 16: Scarborough (Me.) Historical Society; p. 17: Bumble Bee Foods, LLC, and reproduced with permission; p. 19: photo courtesy of Mark Kitching and recipe from *Mrs. Kitching's Smith Island Cookbook* by Frances Kitching and Susan Stiles Dowell, Schiffer Publishing, © 2011; p. 20: photo and recipe courtesy of Karen Colvin; p. 25: postcard courtesy of Elsie Foy/Aunt Carrie's; p. 27: Michael Derr/Southern R.I. Media Group; p. 43: photo and recipe courtesy of Todd Blount/Blount Fine Foods; p. 53: Evelyn DuPont and Gary McWhirter; pp. 78, 89, 100, 112, and 119: beach profiles by Kate LeBlanc; p. 80: Evan Deary; p. 90: recipe courtesy of Jasper White; p. 91: Captain Frosty's; p. 109: Rodney Laughton; p. 121: courtesy of Danny Smith; pp. 124–25: lyrics and chords for "One Clam Cake" courtesy of Marina Campbell (Jon Campbell recordings available from ms.marinac@gmail.com); p. 126: Renee Bessette; p. 132: cartoon © Don Bousquet; p. 133: photo by Jim M. Wyman; p. 134: Sean Fate/Wachapreague Volunteer Fire Co.; p. 137: Evelyn Shotwell/Chincoteague Chamber of Commerce; p. 139: Cheryl Drozdz; p. 163: author photo by Jim M. Wyman.

About the Author

Carolyn Wyman is the author of seven previous food books, including *The Great American Chocolate Chip Cookie Book*, *The Great Philly Cheesesteak Book*, *Better Than Homemade*, *SPAM: A Biography*, and *Jell-O: A Biography*. She has also written for Thrillist, BuzzFeed, the *New York Times*, the *Los Angeles Times*, and the *Philadelphia Inquirer*, and has defended her beloved fatty  foods on *Fresh Air*, *Morning Edition*, CNN, the Food Network, *Fox and Friends*, and the *Rosie O'Donnell Show*. She was weaned on clam cakes and stuffies and still has Del's and coffee milk running through her veins. Learn more at www.carolynwyman.com.